A Gospel Pageant

A Gospel Pageant

A Reader's Guide to the Book of Revelation

Allan Chapple

RESOURCE *Publications* · Eugene, Oregon

A GOSPEL PAGEANT
A Reader's Guide to the Book of Revelation

Resource Publications
An Imprint of Wipf and Stock Publishers
199 W. 8th Ave., Suite 3
Eugene, OR 97401

www.wipfandstock.com

ISBN 13: 978-1-4982-2984-5

Manufactured in the U.S.A.

Contents

Preface

An earlier version of this book was published in 2013 by Mosaic Press in Australia. Not long afterwards, the publisher went out of business. (I don't think my book was the problem!) I continued to be contacted by people wanting to purchase copies, because it seemed that the book was meeting a need and doing what I hoped it would do: that is, getting people into the book of Revelation in a way that helped them get the message. I had encouraging feedback not only from individuals who had read it, but also from several Bible study groups who used it as a guide. So eventually I decided that I should do what these people were urging me to do, and look for someone to bring it back into print. This eventually led me to Wipf & Stock, who kindly agreed to publish the book.

What you have in your hands is not just a reprint of the original book. As I read through it again, it quickly became obvious that it would be improved with a bit of tweaking. So I have worked through it carefully, making numerous changes intended to make it clearer. Although quite a few of these have involved adding some extra sentences or even a paragraph or two, I have resisted the temptation to expand the book as a whole. I am convinced that it needs to be brief if it is to give a big-picture view of the message of Revelation and thus to encourage you to read it for yourself. As you do, I hope that the changes I have made to this guidebook will help you to see more clearly what lies at the heart of that message.

At this point I should tell you why I think this matters. Perhaps you think my aim is to ensure that you get the "right" interpretation of Revelation. In a way, that is true—but that is not because I want you to be "correct" in some abstract sense. What I really want is for you to be gripped by the grandeur of the gospel, that is, to be captivated by the majesty of the sovereign Savior to whom it bears witness and by the immense scope and unsurpassable riches of the salvation and kingdom he is bringing in. The more clearly we see this, the more his glory and grace will lead us to give him the loyal love that he should have from every one of us. And that matters very much indeed!

My thanks to Wipf & Stock for making the publication of the book possible. My thanks to everyone who makes up the Christian community that is Trinity Theological College in Perth, Western Australia. It is a great privilege to belong to a community that keeps giving priority to what matters most: deep and growing devotion to the triune God, our Redeemer and Ruler; steadfast loyalty to the gospel of grace; humble and sacrificial commitment to serving the Lord and his gospel and his people; unhesitating acceptance of the truth of the Bible as the very words of God, and its authority over all of our convictions and conduct; energetic and collaborative pursuit of a truer, deeper grasp of what the Bible teaches in order to make its treasures better known in the church and the world—and much else besides. The result is an environment that stimulates and supports the work that has gone into this book. My thanks especially to Allison, who never complains about the time I spend tapping away at the keyboard or tires of the kind of service that makes it possible for me to keep doing it. My greatest thanks belong to the One who opened my blind eyes to the glory of Jesus Christ and who has never let my weak and wayward devotion slow the torrent of grace he has poured out on me ever since. He should receive your thanks for whatever is true and helpful in this book—and you know who to blame for its defects!

Introduction

CHRISTIANS TEND TO REACT to the book of Revelation in one of three ways. Some are fascinated by it. They are convinced that when decoded rightly, it tells the story of our own time and the End-time. For many of these people, these two times are one and the same. Conversely, some are offended by the book. They find it full of threatening and off-putting things, and are dismayed by what they see as its incompatibility with the rest of the New Testament. But it seems that most Christians are inclined to ignore it. In part, this is because they don't like what the first group does with it; in part, it is because they share the second group's feeling that it isn't like the other books in the New Testament. The net result of all of this is that Revelation does not function in our lives in the way that the rest of the New Testament does. We are all the poorer for this. We need it back in our lives, doing what it is meant to do.

And what is that? As the title of this book indicates, I am convinced that Revelation presents the same gospel we find everywhere else in the New Testament. What is different about it is not its message but the way it presents that message. The content should be familiar—but we haven't seen it dressed up like this before! In fact, if only we can get past how strange this clothing looks, we will find that it is an especially powerful way of presenting the truths of the gospel.

How does this book help us to get Revelation back into our lives? By encouraging us to read it! That is why it is called a "reader's guide." What does this mean? First of all, it indicates that this not a commentary. It does not attempt to explain everything in Revelation. Instead, it is interested in the big picture: it focuses on the main features of the book rather than all the details. So it is quite selective: it simply passes over items in the text that I don't think are primary. But every now and then, we will slow right down and linger over a particular passage, doing our best to work out exactly what it means. There are two reasons for this. One is that these passages can be treated as case-studies. By noting how we analyze them, you will see how you can go about interpreting the rest of the book. Secondly, these passages are especially important for getting the message of Revelation. They are more central and important than passages we pass through quickly or pass over altogether.

So my aim in writing this guidebook is to get you into Revelation, confident that careful, prayerful reading will enable you to get the message. I am convinced that the more often we read Revelation in this way, the clearer its message will become. This doesn't mean that we don't need commentaries. In fact, the more we read Revelation, we might become less sure about some of the details—and thus more aware of how commentaries can help us. But we mustn't turn to the commentaries too soon. They will be of most help once we have read carefully through Revelation often enough to be clear about its basic message—and often enough to be stumped by some of the details.

Here are my suggestions about how to use this guidebook. Each of its chapters begins by indicating what part of Revelation it discusses. You will find it helpful to read this section before you read the chapter itself. And you will get more out of each chapter if you have your Bible open at the relevant passage, so that you can follow what is being said about particular verses or sections. The translation I will be quoting here is the NIV2011, but any mainstream translation will do fine. Once you have finished the chapter, you will find it helpful to re-read the relevant section of Revelation, using the questions at the end of the chapter to guide you.

As you go through Revelation with this guidebook, my aim is to make sure that the big picture becomes clearer and clearer for you. If it really is a gospel pageant, then you should find that it keeps drawing attention especially to the glory and grace of Jesus as Lord and Savior, to our desperate need for salvation and all that he has done in his death and resurrection to win it for us, and to his coming in triumph to bring this salvation to its glorious completion. There will also be other things it presents along the way, and there will be times when you are not sure what to make of what it says. What you should try to do at these points is to keep giving most attention to the big truths, without either ignoring the other things or letting them take over. Each of the chapters in this book has been written with the aim of helping you to get this balance right.

The most important thing of all is to read Revelation prayerfully. One thing you can be very sure about is that its Author is always available to help you get the message. If you are not sure what to say, here is a prayer you could use before you start reading:

Dear Father,

Thank you for giving us this testimony by John to "the word of God and the testimony of Jesus Christ." Please help me to read it carefully and thoughtfully, so that I see exactly what it is saying. And please teach me by your Spirit as I do so, so that its message may grip me and shape me in all of the ways you intend it to do. Please grant especially that the more I read it, the more I will be gripped by the truth and power of the gospel, the more I will be grateful for your great salvation, and the more I will grow in my love for your Son and my loyalty to him.

I ask you this in Jesus' name, Amen.

And now, if you are ready, let us begin the great adventure of working our way through the book of Revelation.

Chapter 1

Stop, Look, and Listen!
Revelation 1:1—3:22

WHO WOULD HAVE THOUGHT that a Coke bottle could cause so much trouble? If you have seen the movie, *The Gods Must Be Crazy*, you will probably remember the problems the Coke bottle caused when it fell from the sky into the Bushmen's camp in the Kalahari desert. The point is a simple one: if you don't know what it is, you don't know what to do with it! This applies to the book of Revelation as well as to Coke bottles. This means that our first task is to discover what this book is. Until we find out the answer, we won't know what we are meant to do with it. And if we don't know that, we might end up misusing it, by trying to make it do something it isn't meant to do. Unfortunately, this happens quite often with Revelation. Yet there is really no excuse for misusing it, for John begins his book by telling us exactly what it is. But the answer isn't a simple one.

Stop: What did John write?

This is a book which has four sides to its character. Can you see how John tells us this in the first four verses? (We discover the same four truths about the character of this book in 22:6–21. Once you have seen them in 1:1–4, it is not difficult to find them at the end of the book as well.) Our job at this point is to work our way patiently through each of these four verses, to see what they tell us about the message and purpose of Revelation.

In the first verse John tells us that this book is a *revelation*. That is why it bears this name. What is a "revelation"? It is what happens when a fog lifts. When you are in a thick fog it is very difficult to see anything around you, no matter how hard you look. But when the air clears, your eyes can do their job again. The disappearance of the fog reveals what is there—what used to be invisible can now be seen. In a similar way, God discloses truths that we couldn't work out by ourselves.

> The secret things belong to the LORD our God, but the things revealed belong to us and to our children forever . . . (Deut 29:29)

When God reveals something, he makes known what we didn't know and couldn't have known. That is what the book of Revelation is doing.

Verse 1 makes it clear that this is no ordinary revelation—if there could be such a thing! Did you note the careful chain of transmission by which God gives this revelation to his servants? It goes from God to Jesus Christ to his angel to his servant John and then to God's servants. What could be so special, that God took such steps to reveal it to us? What God is disclosing to us in this book is "what must soon take place." What is this? Why "must" it take place? And how soon is "soon"?

We don't have to read much further before we discover what this is referring to. In verse 7 we read that Jesus Christ is returning. And second-time readers of this book know that it ends with Jesus' words, "I am coming soon" (22:7, 12, 20). This is what must happen soon. But why must it happen? What makes his return necessary? It is because the Lord Jesus has begun something in his death and resurrection that is not yet complete. He must return to bring in his great salvation in all its fulness. What must take place soon is the return of the redeeming, resurrected, and reigning Lord. He is "the firstborn from the dead" (1:5)—so he must return to raise all dead believers to new and glorious life. He is "the ruler of the kings of the earth" (1:5)—yet most of the people on earth and their rulers do not acknowledge him, so he must return to be acclaimed as the Lord of all. But how can this be "soon," when some two thousand years have passed since John wrote these words?—and we are still waiting! We will come back to this important question when we investigate verse 3.

In verse 2 we find that this book is a *testimony*. Whose testimony is it? It is by a servant of Jesus Christ named John (v.1). And who is he? He tells us in verse 9. He is the "brother" of his readers. This means that he is a fellow-believer, a member with them of God's great family. He then indicates three things that he shares with them: "the suffering and kingdom and patient endurance that are ours in Jesus." These are not three separate things, for John uses "the" only once. He is referring to the suffering-and-kingdom-and-patient-endurance that they all share. This is meant to be a hint about what we should look for as we read this book. It will disclose various ways in which Christians suffer in this world. Yet it will also remind us often that God is in charge (the "kingdom")—so even though we suffer, we could not be safer! And it will urge us to endure: to be steadfast in our loyalty to the Lord Jesus and his gospel (note especially 13:10; 14:12).

What is John testifying about? He is giving eyewitness testimony: he is telling us what he saw. And what was that? He says that he saw "the word of God and the testimony of Jesus Christ." Surely this is a mistake! Doesn't he mean that he *heard* these things? How can you *see* a word? I'm not completely sure—but this is something we meet often enough in the Old Testament prophets. Take Isaiah, for example. His book begins with these words: "The vision concerning Judah and Jerusalem that Isaiah son of Amoz saw" (Isa 1:1). But what follows is not a picture, but words: "Hear me, you heavens! Listen, earth! For the LORD has spoken . . ." (1:2). A bit later, we read these words: "A prophecy against Babylon that Isaiah son of Amoz saw" (Isa 13:1). Once again, what follows is the words that Isaiah was given to speak, the words that make up his prophecy.

It seems that if you are a prophet, you can see a word! Although it is hard to be sure how this happened with the prophets, the basic idea is not really all that strange. We are familiar with the idea of "picture-language" or "word-pictures." This is what we are dealing with, for example, when John the Baptizer sees Jesus and calls him, "the Lamb of God" (John 1:29, 36). In the book of Revelation, this kind of language comes to life. When this John sees Jesus, he *is* a Lamb (5:6). (He also appears in other forms in subsequent visions.) This is what is happening throughout the book, as John sees word-pictures that have sprung to life. The visions of Revelation are mobile metaphors. It would therefore be a mistake to read it in a literalistic way. In this book, we are seeing the truth in pictures. So the Lord Jesus is not a slain Lamb, and nor does he actually look like one. But when we see him as a Lamb, we are being reminded of one aspect of the truth about who he is and what he has done for us. And the same applies to the other occasions on which we see him in this book. Each of the forms in which he appears tells us something about what he is like. Their job is not to tell us about his appearance but about his character and status and roles. What they show us is not what he looks like but what he is like. This applies also to all of the other figures we see in this book, such as the dragon and the beasts in chapters 12 and 13.

When John says that he saw "the word of God and the testimony of Jesus Christ," what is he referring to? In the New Testament, "the word of God" is generally a reference to the gospel. This fits what we read in this book. Those who have been martyred for the word of God (6:9; 20:4) will be those whose loyalty to the gospel has cost them their lives. And when John says that he was on the island of Patmos "because of the word of God" (1:9), he most likely means that he was there to do gospel-work: that is, evangelism and church-planting. So when he saw the word of God, this was not revealing something he didn't know. It was not a presentation of new truth, but a new presentation of known truth. What is new about this book is not the content but the form in which John encounters it. His visions showed him the gospel. Time and again, he would have been thinking, "I already knew this—but I just hadn't seen it this way before!" And that is what should happen to us as we work our way through the book. What we are seeing is a gospel pageant, a series of vivid and dramatic tableaus that depict the great truths of the gospel in a gripping and powerful way. It is as though the apostles' message was taken to the Disney studios and turned into an animated movie. Their word-pictures have sprung into life; their metaphors have become mobile.

What about "the testimony of Jesus Christ"? What does this mean? It could mean testimony about Jesus Christ—the testimony that his people give to him. This certainly fits what we read elsewhere in the book (6:9; 12:11; 17:6; 20:4). Equally, it could mean testimony by Jesus Christ—the testimony that he himself gives. Hence verse 5, where John tells us that Jesus is "the faithful witness." And at the end of the book Jesus describes himself as "he who testifies to these things" (22:20). But whether the testimony is to Jesus Christ or by Jesus Christ, the gospel is at its heart. In giving their testimony to Jesus, people hold forth the gospel (note 6:9; 20:4). In giving his testimony, Jesus does the same. The sequence in 1:5 suggests that Jesus was the faithful witness in his ministry and his death. This matches what we read in John's Gospel, where we find that Jesus the witness spoke God's words (John 3:32–34), and testified to the truth (John 18:37)—especially the truth about himself and his saving mission (John 8:12–18). Just a few verses before 22:20, Jesus says that he has sent his angel to give "this testimony" to the churches (22:16). In light of 1:1, this makes best sense as a reference to the book itself. And as we have just seen, this is a gospel pageant. So "the testimony of Jesus Christ" turns out to be closely connected in meaning to "the word of God"— both point us to the gospel. In verse 2, then, John is telling us that the truths of the gospel were presented to him in visionary form.

Verse 3 tells us that this book is a *prophecy*. And what does this word mean? Most people think of it as a forecast, a prediction of something in the future. This certainly fits some of what the Bible calls "prophecy," which does announce what is going to happen (see 1 Pet 1:10–12, for example). But a great deal of biblical prophecy refers to the past and the present rather than the future. What makes it prophecy is not where it is focused, what time-period it refers to, but where it comes from. A prophecy is God's message given through a human messenger—God's words in human words (2 Pet 1:21). Indeed, we can say that a "prophecy" (v.3) is a "revelation" (v.1) in a "testimony" (v.2)!

What are we meant to do with this prophecy? Verse 3 gives us two answers to this question. The first is that unlike the prophecy given to Daniel (Dan 12:4, 9), for example, this one is to be made public. This will happen as the book is read out and its contents are heard. Even though we usually encounter its message by reading it, this is a book that was intended to be read aloud. Remembering this will help the book to have its intended impact on us. Whether we read it or hear it, what are we meant to do with its contents? If Revelation was just a forecast of the future, then all we could do with it is to wait until what it predicts actually happens. But a literal translation of verse 3 says that we are meant to "keep" what is written in it. This is a little surprising, for we would normally expect to find "keep" attached to something else that we find in our Bibles. Keeping is what we are meant to do with command-ments. So if we read this book rightly, we will find that it is not just giving us information, satisfying our curiosity about the future. Revelation is not some Christian version of a horoscope! Rather, it is God addressing us with a compelling and authoritative message which we must heed and obey. Second-time readers of the book will think of such things as the way it calls for perseverance on our part (13:10; 14:12).

John gives a sense of urgency to all of this by saying that "the time is near." What does he mean by this? And what does he mean by "what must soon take place" (v.1)? How soon is "soon"—and how near is "near"? Surely two thousand years cannot count as either soon or near—and we are still waiting! Do we just have to accept that the New Testament got it wrong? Many people think so, but this is only because they misunderstand what is happening here. When John said these things he was not so much looking forwards as looking backwards. He was not looking at what is still to come and estimating (wrongly!) that there's only a little way to go. Instead, he was looking at what had just happened and recognizing that what remains is bound to come. By saying "soon" and "near," he was not really making a chronological calculation about how close the Lord's return was. Rather, he was making a theological affirmation about how weighty the Lord's death and resurrection were. These great events must be seen as the promised End arriving early, before the End! Or we can say that the End began at Easter. Either way, when Christian hope sets its eyes on the future, it has its feet planted in the past. And now that the End has been established, it is straining towards completion. Because of what the Lord Jesus has done already, what he is yet to do is pushing hard to burst into the present. It *must* happen, because it belongs with what has happened. It is the necessary completion of what has already been done for us. And it must happen *soon*. One way of understanding this is to think of Jesus' past work and his coming work as like the two sides of a spring-loaded trap. There is a powerful pressure pulling them together, which means that they can only be held apart by an even stronger force. As soon as the trap is sprung, the two sides come together immediately and with great force. When the power separating them is released, there is no waiting. That is why such devices are used as traps. So it is with Jesus' return. God is holding it back, widening the gap back to Jesus' death and resurrection, because he is a patient Savior (2 Pet 3:9). But as soon as he stops doing this, the End will happen at once. It is that near!

In verse 4 we discover that this book is a *letter*. If it had started with this verse, it would have been called "Asians"! That is because its wording—"John, to the seven churches in . . . Asia"—follows the same pattern as that of Paul's letters to his churches. So the letter which begins, "Paul . . . to the churches in Galatia," is known as "Galatians."

You will notice that I have just omitted several words from verse 4. This is because our English Bibles have added the words, "the province of . . ." What John wrote was, "to the seven churches in Asia." But imagine what most readers would do without the additional words in our Bibles. We would think, "There's the Japanese church, the Chinese church, the Korean church, the Vietnamese church . . ." We would quickly reach a total greater than seven, and would then be puzzled as to why John thought that there were only seven Asian churches. That is because we unconsciously assume that what Revelation's words suggest to us is what they really mean. Unless our Bibles added these extra words, we would be likely to think that "Asia" means what it means in our world. We might never get around to asking, "What did this word mean in their world: that is, what did it mean to John and his churches?" For them, "Asia" was one of the provinces that made up the Roman Empire. It covered roughly the western third of modern Turkey. This alerts us to an extremely important principle. As we read this book, we must keep telling ourselves, "This means what it meant to them." After all, it was written in their language (Greek), not ours. And as we will see in the next few pages, it addresses their situation, not ours, and assumes their background, not ours. So we need to keep reminding ourselves that the meaning of what John tells us comes from the first century Middle East, not the twenty-first century West. This doesn't apply only to what "Asia" means; it applies to the book as a whole. So the weird locusts in chapter 9 cannot be helicopter-gunships, as one modern interpreter claims. That can't be right, because it leaves John and his churches out of the picture and implies that we are the only readers of this book who count.

All of this gives us another item to add to the chain of transmission we saw in verse 1. The revelation from God comes through John to God's servants. In the first place, this refers to the believers who make up the seven Asian churches. Only then does it include us. God is speaking to us now in what he said to them then. The message of Revelation is *for* us and *for* all of God's people in every place and time—but it was not given *to* us; it was sent to them. In order to hear what God is saying to us, we must first hear what he was saying to them. Only when we have heard the message against that background can we bring it across into our own context. And that is, of course, exactly the same as the way we work out what apostolic letters like Galatians are saying to us.

So far we have been looking at ways in which Revelation is like other New Testament books such as Galatians. Now it is time to notice one important way in which the two are different. This concerns their introductions. In the New Testament letters the introductions are intended to give the readers an indication of what to look out for as they read the rest of the letter. In Galatians, the introduction consists of five brief verses, but in Revelation it is almost twice as long—seventy-five Greek words in Galatians as against one hundred and thirty in Revelation (1:4–8). What does John's introduction draw our attention to? It emphasizes the majesty of God and the glory of Jesus Christ. The Father is presented as the eternal God. His existence covers past, present, and future—he was, and is, and is to come (vv.4, 8). He is the beginning and the end—the Alpha and Omega (v.8: these are the first and last letters of the Greek alphabet). He is also acknowledged as the sovereign God: he is enthroned (v.4), and he is the Almighty (v.8). The glory of Jesus Christ is seen in who he is (v.5a), what he has done (vv.5b–6), and what he will do (v.7). By this unusually lengthy introduction John is telling his readers to make sure that they maintain the right focus while they read his book. If we don't keep on being confronted by the majesty and sovereignty of the eternal God and the glory and grace of Jesus Christ, then we are not reading the book rightly.

I wonder if you have noticed the pattern in these first four verses as they tell us what the book is. The first and third are about something that God has done, while the second and fourth are about what John has done. God has given a revelation and a prophecy; John has given his testimony and written a letter. So, like the rest of Scripture, this book has both a divine side and a human side—it comes from God, and it comes also from John. It is God's word in John's words.

Why did John write this letter-testimony? It is because of something that happened to him one Sunday on the island of Patmos (1:9–11). And just what did happen to him on that momentous day? We need to pay careful attention to what he tells us, for if we can understand this first section of his testimony, then we stand a better chance of understanding the rest of the book.

Look: What did John see?

The remarkable experience to which he testifies began when he heard someone speaking to him (1:10–11). This was no ordinary voice, for it was "like a trumpet." When John turned around to see who this could be, he saw a human-like figure standing amidst seven golden lampstands (1:12–16). Yet the sight of this figure was so overwhelming, that John collapsed (1:17). The figure then touched John and spoke to him again (1:17–20). What is the meaning of this vision? Who did John hear and see?

We must be careful not to jump to conclusions here. We need to make sure that we notice exactly what John tells us, so that we get the message he intended to communicate. So, what exactly did he see? He saw someone "like a son of man" (v.13)—which is a biblical way of saying, "a figure that looks human." (We see this from its use in Ezekiel 1:26 and Daniel 7:13, where there is an obvious contrast between this figure and weird or fearsome creatures that are quite unlike any human being.) This figure is dressed like a contestant in Miss World, wearing a floor-length robe, with a golden sash around the chest (v.13). Yet John refers to the figure as a male ("his feet," "his chest," and so on). In that world, there was obviously nothing strange about a man being dressed like this. This reminds us at once that we have to apply the principle, "it means what it meant to them." We must ask the question, who wore such robes and sashes in *that* society? This clothing tells us that John is seeing a high-status dignitary. This is how Israel's priests were dressed (Exod 28:31–35, 39–41). It was also how kings and royal officials dressed (Gen 41:42; 1 Sam 18:4; 1 Kgs 22:10; Isa 22:15, 20–21; John 19:2–3). The point is that John is seeing someone whose rank or status is very high indeed. This is someone great, someone very important.

The next thing we need to notice is all the ways in which this human figure is not a normal human being. What John heard was "a loud voice like a trumpet" (v.10), or like a torrent of water (v.15). The speaker's general appearance is radiant and dazzling: his hair is pure white; his eyes are like blazing fire; his feet are like glowing bronze; and his face shines like the sun (vv.14–16). In some ways, this is like visions the prophets had of God (Ezek 1:26–28; 43:2; Dan 7:9); in other ways, it is like their visions of angels (Ezek 40:3; Dan 10:5–6; cf. Matt 28:3). This tells us that John is seeing and hearing a heavenly being. That is why he falls prostrate before him (v.17a; cf. 19:10; 22:8). That is also why he needs to be told, "Do not be afraid" (v.17b)—which is usually the first thing that heavenly beings have to say to the people they meet (Matt 28:5; Luke 1:13, 30: 2:10; John 6:20; Acts 18:9).

It is not until the figure speaks a second time that we discover who he really is. Although Lazarus and a few other people in the Bible could have said, "I was dead," only one person was in a position to add, "I am alive for ever and ever!" (v.18). Yes, John is seeing the risen and exalted Jesus in his heavenly glory. He is truly human: "I was dead" (v.18). Yet he is also truly God: "I am the First and the Last" (v.17; cf. v.8). And he is the living Lord: "I am alive for ever and ever! And I hold the keys of death and Hades" (v.18).

What do we learn from this first vision which might help us interpret the other visions John is going to describe? We can draw four principles from this passage. The first is that the words explain the pictures. It was because of what Jesus said to him that John knew that it was Jesus he was seeing. What is said explains what is seen. The second principle is that the pictures look familiar to John and his churches. What John describes has two sources: it combines echoes of their Scripture (our Old Testament) and expressions of their culture. As we have learned already, it means what it meant to them. The third principle is that no one vision reveals everything. Second-time readers of the book know that this is not the only time John sees the Lord Jesus, and each time he sees him he looks quite different. So he is going to see him as a slain but enthroned Lamb (5:6), as a newborn infant (12:6), as a crowned reaper seated on a cloud (14:14), and as a warrior-king seated on a horse (19:11–16). Each vision draws attention to some aspects of Jesus' person and work, but none of these visions tells us everything about him. How could it? The fourth and last principle is that a vision is a vision, not a video. John is not seeing a documentary, showing us historical events in advance. He is seeing word-pictures that have sprung to life, metaphors that have become mobile.

Listen: What did John hear?

What message did the Lord Jesus have for John? He was told to write down what he saw and send it to the seven churches (1:11). And he was given a separate message for each of these churches (2:1–3:22). What are we intended to learn from these letters?

We should begin by noting that there is an underlying pattern that each message follows quite closely.

- *To the angel of the church in . . . write* (2:1, 8, 12, 18; 3:1, 7, 14).

- *These are the words of . . .* (2:1, 8, 12, 18; 3:1, 7, 14). In all but the sixth and seventh letters, Jesus identifies himself by referring to some element of the vision John reports in 1:12–18. In the message to Philadelphia, his words look ahead to 6:9 and 19:11 and back to Isaiah 22:22. In that to Laodicea, they look back in part to 1:5.

- *I know . . .* (2:2, 9, 13, 19; 3:1, 8, 15). All except 2:9 and 2:13 have *I know your deeds . . .*

- *Whoever has ears, let them hear what the Spirit says to the churches* (2:7, 11, 17, 29; 3:6, 13, 22).

- *To the one who is victorious, I will give . . .* (2:7, 17; 3:21). This formula is slightly varied in 2:11, 26; 3:5, 12. In the fourth, fifth, sixth, and seventh letters it precedes the previous item.

What do we learn from this pattern, and from the contents of each of the seven messages? First, we note that the messages are addressed to the "angel" of each of the churches. While it is difficult to be sure what this means, it does not indicate that these messages are private, meant only for church leaders, for example. It is clear from their wording that each message is intended to reach the whole church to which it is addressed. Writing to the angel of the church in Ephesus amounts to writing to all the members of that church. Just before he gives these messages, the Lord Jesus reveals that the angels of these churches are represented by the seven stars he is seen holding in his right hand (1:16, 20). This is probably meant to remind the hearers of Jesus' promise that his sheep are securely held in his grasp, and that no one can snatch them out of his hand (John 10:28). The churches may be hard-pressed and under threat—but they are also very secure.

Secondly, the Lord Jesus identifies himself in a way that makes this first vision extremely important. What John sees and hears (1:12–18) has great significance for all of the churches. No matter what he sees and reports from this point on, and no matter how threatening or terrible it is, the Lord Jesus has been seen in his heavenly glory as the living Lord. In all of their problems and perils, these hard-pressed believers can hold fast to him, knowing that he has triumphed and that he will triumph. To belong to him is to be secure indeed.

Thirdly, the bulk of each message follows Jesus' affirmation that he knows the condition and circumstances of the church concerned. This means that the messages are targeted: what they say is exactly what each church needs to hear. It also means that the rest of the book addresses the needs and problems of these seven churches. None of it is beside the point or merely of general interest; all of it speaks directly to their situation. And what is that situation? What was happening in and to these churches?

The churches were experiencing problems that came from two sides—from inside and from outside. So the church in Ephesus was plagued by an internal problem. Its members had abandoned the love they had at first and have fallen a long way (2:4–5). The church in Smyrna, by contrast, faced external threats. They had endured afflictions (2:9), and now were about to suffer severe persecution (2:10). The church in Pergamum was challenged on both fronts: one of their members has been martyred (2:13), and some of them have accepted false teaching and the practices that go with it (2:14–15).

The problems confronting them had two sources—they came from human agents, and they came from Satan. From one angle, the churches were threatened by the Nicolaitans (2:6, 15), by persecutors, some of whom were killers (2:10, 13), by those who hold to Balaam's teaching (2:14), and by "Jezebel" and those who follow her teaching (2:20, 24). But behind and underneath the human opposition, working in and through it, was the opposition of Satan (2:10, 13, 24). In their cities, he has his synagogues (2:9; 3:9) and his throne (2:13).

The problems they faced were of two types—error and terror, trickery and tyranny. Their enemies were misleading them and mistreating them. They were facing the evil one in his twin roles as a liar and a murderer (John 8:44). He disguises himself as an angel of light (2 Cor 11:14), and he prowls around like a lion looking for prey (1 Pet 5:8). So they were troubled by fraud: by false apostles (2:2), false Jews (2:9; 3:9), and false prophets (2:14, 20). And they were threatened by force: by imprisonment (2:10) and martyrdom (2:10, 13).

Fourthly, the hearers of each message are told that they should pay attention to all of the messages: "let them hear what the Spirit says to the churches." Although each one speaks about the specific issues facing the church concerned, there is a sense in which these messages are relevant to all of these churches. In part, this reflects the fact that because they are in the same general area ("Asia"), what affects one is likely to affect others. So, for example, there are "Nicolaitans" in two of the churches (2:6, 15), and two are threatened by "a synagogue of Satan" (2:9; 3:9). But it also reflects the fact that the tests facing them are "what is common to mankind" (1 Cor 10:13). The Bible makes it clear that all churches in all places and times are under pressure from the world, the flesh, and the Devil. So the members of all seven churches have something to learn from what the Lord says to each one of them. And this applies to us too—despite all the ways in which we differ from them, what Jesus says to these seven churches also speaks to us.

Fifthly, specific blessings are promised to those who are victorious. These promises raise two questions. First, how does one become "victorious"? And secondly, when will the victory gift—the promised blessing—be received? We can only read on, waiting to see if the rest of the book will answer these questions.

The Lord Jesus has now addressed each of the seven churches in Asia. His message to each one is right on target, directly addressing their needs and problems. Each message is also of use to the other churches—what Jesus says to each one is what the Spirit is saying to them all. So what else is there? What still needs to be said? What does the rest of Revelation do?

Questions for Reading 1:1–3:22 Again

1. According to John, what kind of book is Revelation? How does the answer he gives help us to approach the book the right way?

2. What do we learn from 1:11–20 about how to read visions?

3. What kinds of trouble faced the seven churches?

4. What were the churches meant to learn from Jesus' seven messages?

Chapter 2

The Heavenly Perspective
Revelation 4:1—7:17

FOR QUITE SOME TIME, John has been listening (1:17–3:22). Then as soon as Jesus completes his messages to the seven churches, another vision begins. But this one starts not with sound but with sight. What John sees this time is a door in heaven, and it is open (4:1a). Then he hears the same booming voice he heard at the beginning of the first vision (4:1b; cf. 1:10). This is the Lord Jesus summoning him to come up into heaven, so that he can show him "what must take place after this." This tells us that John is going to see the future. But this is not just any future. It is not what *will* take place, but what *must* take place. What makes these things necessary is what has happened already. John is going to see the future that the past has made essential—the End that began at Easter. That is, he is going to see how what Jesus has already established will be completed. What he has done for us in his death and resurrection must come to its glorious fulfillment. This is what must take place—and this is what John will see.

Before we follow John into heaven, this is a good place to register two important things about this book. The first concerns its shape. There are two main structure-markers in the book. The first is the way the main sights and sounds are grouped in sevens, like the messages John has just received (2:1–3:22). The next such group is the seals that are broken off a scroll (5:1–8:1), and this sequence introduces the seven trumpets (8:2–11:18) . . . and so on. The second structure-marker is the periodic appearance of heavenly openings, like this one. These divide the book into its main sections. The next is in 11:19, where God's temple is open. Then in 15:5, the temple or tabernacle is open. Finally, in 19:11 heaven itself is standing open. Each of these openings is preceded by an outburst of praise which brings the previous section to an end. So 11:15–18 ends the section which begins in 4:1; 15:3–4 ends that which begins in 11:19; and 19:1–8 ends that which begins in 15:5. Thus, when we exclude the introduction (1:1–8) and conclusion (22:6–21), Revelation is made up of five visions. Vision 1 takes us from 1:9 to 3:22; Vision 2 from 4:1 to 11:18; Vision 3 from 11:19 to 15:4; Vision 4 from 15:5 to 19:10; and Vision 5 from 19:11 to 22:5.

We are alerted to a second feature of Revelation by the way John is allowed into heaven. Such visits, and the heavenly visions the visitor experiences, are a feature of writings that were quite common amongst Jewish people around the time of the New Testament. These are known as apocalyptic writings. These report visions or dreams in which the seer encounters angels and other heavenly beings, mysterious numbers, symbolic colors, upheavals in the physical environment, talking beasts which combine the features of several different animals, and so on. People who were familiar with these writings would not have found Revelation the least bit unusual. All the things about it that seem strange to us were common features of apocalyptic works. Here is an example:

> On the second night I had a dream, and behold, there came up from the sea an eagle that had twelve feathered wings and three heads. And I looked, and behold, he spread his wings over all the earth, and all the winds of heaven blew upon him, and the clouds were gathered about him. And I looked, and out of his wings there grew opposing wings; but they became little, puny wings. But his heads were at rest; the middle head was larger than the other heads, but it also was at rest with them. And I looked, and behold, the eagle flew with his wings, to

reign over the earth and over those who dwell in it . . .
Then I heard a voice saying to me, "Look before you and
consider what you see." And I looked, and behold, a crea-
ture like a lion was aroused out of the forest, roaring, and
I heard how he uttered a man's voice to the eagle, and
spoke, saying, "Listen and I will speak to you . . ." . . . After seven days I dreamed a dream in the night; and
behold, a wind arose from the sea and stirred up all its
waves. And I looked, and behold, this wind made something like the figure of a man come up out of the heart
of the sea. And I looked, and behold, that man flew with
the clouds of heaven; and wherever he turned his face to
look, everything under his gaze trembled, and whenever
his voice issued from his mouth, all who heard his voice
melted as wax melts when it feels the fire. After this I
looked, and behold, an innumerable multitude of men
were gathered together from the four winds of heaven to
make war against the man who came up out of the sea.

This comes from an apocalyptic writing called the Fourth
Book of Ezra—but it sounds as though it could be from Revelation, doesn't it? What this tells us is that God communicated with
John and his churches in a way that was familiar to them. From
one perspective, this is a new way of presenting the truth of the
gospel—new in that the rest of the New Testament doesn't make
much use of it. But from another perspective, this isn't new. For
them, it was a known way of speaking about God and his purposes. Once again, we are reminded that "it means what it meant
to them."

Heaven's Lord: the Throne at the center

What happens when John enters heaven? We are expecting him
to see the future: "what must take place after this" (4:1). Yet it is
not the future that he sees, but the throne—he finds himself in the
imperial throne-room! The first thing he sees is a throne with the
monarch seated on it (4:2). The sight is dazzling (4:3, 5b–6a) and
the sounds are awesome (4:5a). Then he sees the royal courtiers

(4:4, 6b–7). And then he hears what the courtiers are saying about the Emperor (4:8–11). This must have had a huge impact on John. Even now, with only his words to go by, we can sense something of the way it would have affected him. Why did God give him this experience? What does it all mean?

We begin where John did, with the throne: "there before me was a throne in heaven" (4:2). The New Testament uses the word "throne" sixty-two times. Of these, forty-seven are in Revelation, with seventeen in chapters 4 and 5. Clearly, John's admission into heaven is meant to focus our attention on God's royal majesty and sovereignty. What John and his churches need most is not to know what the future holds but to know who holds the future. They are going to see what must take place soon (1:1; 4:1)—but even more important than that is knowing who is in control. The God of heaven is sovereign in the cosmos. He is not just a spectator; he rules! The fundamental fact behind, underneath, and above all other reality is the lordship, the sovereignty, of God. To seven hard-pressed churches, John's vision of the heavenly Ruler comes as very good news. The intended effect of this vision is much the same as that of John's first one (1:12–20). It is to reassure the churches that they belong to a great Sovereign, a mighty Lord—and that, belonging to him, they are very secure.

Now we turn our attention to the sights and sounds that came flooding in upon John's senses (4:2–11). Is this what heaven looks like? No, for this is just like John's vision of the Lord Jesus: it tells us what heaven is like, not what it looks like. Does God actually sit on a throne? No, for he doesn't have a body! But is he a great Ruler? Yes, indeed! So what is being revealed here is not the appearance of heaven but its character. And as was the case with the first vision, this revelation reflects both their Scripture and their culture. What John reports echoes what we read in Isaiah 6, Ezekiel 1, and Daniel 7. It also reflects what people are likely to have known about the imperial court. So what is John's vision telling us about heavenly reality?

Just before we answer this question, it is worth pausing to learn something important from a nursery-rhyme. I am thinking of these words:

> Pussy cat, pussy cat, where have you been? I've been to London, to visit the Queen.
>
> Pussy cat, pussy cat, what did you there? I frightened a little mouse under her chair.

And how does this help us? By warning us against a big mistake. It is possible to be in the presence of royalty, but instead of being focused on the person on the throne I can be distracted by a mouse! When I am reading this report of what John saw and heard, I have to be careful not to be distracted by the little things. If he brings me with him into the imperial throne-room, then I should be giving my attention above all to the Emperor. And that is certainly where John wants us to focus, for he not only begins there (4:2–3) but also makes it clear that all of the activity in the throne-room is centered on the One who is enthroned (4:4–11). Here and in the rest of the book as well, I must make sure I avoid repeating the mistake of the distracted cat. I cannot afford to be preoccupied with the mice so that I end up missing what really matters.

And that brings us back to the question of what this vision is meant to tell us about heavenly reality. The most important thing we learn is that God is at the center of it all. It is his being what he is that makes heaven what it is. And what is he? The throne speaks of his absolute sovereignty. The sights and sounds around the throne reflect his awesome majesty. His presence means dazzling beauty (4:3), immense power (4:5a), and unapproachable purity (4:6a). John is seeing a God who is majestic in his glory, might, and holiness.

What do we learn from the royal courtiers, the twenty-four elders and the four living creatures? Our inclination is to wonder about their identity, but John's report directs our attention to their activity: what matters most is not who they are but what they do. They are focused on the throne, and are occupied entirely with giving praise and honor to its occupant. The living creatures acknowledge ceaselessly that the eternal Ruler of all is holy (4:8). The twenty-four elders are equally unceasing in their confession that the sovereign Creator of all is worthy (4:9–11). The glory of God is thus the focus of all attention and activity in heaven.

John already knew all this, of course—but he had never seen it this way before. And why has he been given this vision? As we have seen, the messages for the seven churches show that they are hard-pressed, facing threats of various kinds (2:1–3:22). They are John's partners in "the suffering . . . that [is] ours in Jesus" (1:9). Such pressures always carry with them the danger that we will lose perspective, that is, that we will no longer see things from the right angle. What we need most when we are really struggling is the ability to see our situation from the heavenly perspective. And that is what John has been given, for his own sake and for the sake of his churches. It is as though he (and we with him) is taken into the control tower at a large and busy airport. Normally, we only get to see things there from ground level. From this perspective, such an airport seems to be verging on chaos, with planes, vehicles, people, and luggage going in all directions. It is very difficult to see any overall pattern and order in what is happening. But when seen from the control tower, it all looks quite different. What looks chaotic at ground level is actually under control. What is happening is orderly and coordinated, not random or meaningless. So John and his churches need to get used to seeing things from the heavenly perspective. They need to remember the throne! They must not become preoccupied with what they can see, with what is right in front of them—their hardships and their opposition. That will only breed discouragement and fear. They must keep on reminding themselves that behind their circumstances, under the surface, above their troubles, God rules.

History's Lord: the Lamb at the center

We have gone on John's quick tour of the imperial throne-room—so now do we get to see the future, "what must take place" (4:1)? In a way, we do. It is at this point that John notices a sealed scroll in the Emperor's right hand (5:1). We aren't told what this is—probably because it isn't difficult to work out what is likely to be on a scroll being held by the Emperor while he is seated on his throne. This is bound to be some imperial decree, setting out the Emperor's will for his Empire. So this scroll would tell us what is going to happen—if we could open it. But to his utter dismay, John discovers that no one is fit to do so (5:3-4). His sobbing shows us how terrible it would be if God's purposes were hidden from us. This would leave us hopelessly, terribly lost—we would have no idea where we were or where we should be heading, like people caught in an impenetrable fog that never lifts.

What the devastated John now hears and sees is the prelude to jubilation in heaven. First, he hears something (5:5). One of the elders tells him of the conquering Lion who alone is worthy to unseal the Emperor's scroll. As the Lion from the tribe of Judah, he would remind John and his churches of Genesis 49:9-10. And as the Root of David, he would remind them of Isaiah 11:1-10. In other words, they would recognize this as a reference to the promised Messiah. So they would not be surprised to learn that he has "triumphed." What else would you expect from a mighty King who is even greater than his ancestor David?

What happens next, however, is quite a surprise. John now sees something (5:6)—but it is not a triumphant Lion; it is a slain Lamb! So where has the Lion gone? Nowhere, for John never gets to see a Lion. He is only told about the Lion, but what he sees is a Lamb—and these two are one and the same. Consider what John sees. The Lamb has the marks of death: it looks "as if it had been slain." It also has the marks of deity. It has seven horns—a biblical way of picturing perfect power. It also has seven eyes, picturing perfect knowledge or wisdom. And it is at the center of the imperial throne, indicating divine sovereignty. What John is seeing is not something new—although he hadn't seen it this way before. He is seeing what Paul says about the Messiah: "we preach Christ crucified . . . Christ the power of God and the wisdom of God" (1 Cor 1:23-24). This is also a way of depicting what the Lord Jesus says at the beginning of John's visions: "I am the First and the Last.

I am the Living One; I was dead, and now look, I am alive for ever and ever! And I hold the keys of death and Hades." (1:17–18). The Lion is the Lamb: what we share in Jesus is both the suffering (the Lamb) and the kingdom (the Lion) (1:9).

As soon as John saw the Lamb, it took the scroll from the Emperor's right hand (5:7). This leads the royal courtiers to worship the Lamb (5:8–10). They now add the praises of the redeeming Lamb to their unending praise of the reigning Lord. The imperial throne-room now comes to resemble a three-tiered grandstand, as first the angelic hosts (5:11–12) and then the entire creation (5:13) add their praises to that of the heavenly courtiers.

What is this telling us? It is making three important points. First, when the Lamb takes the scroll, we are reminded that the Lord Jesus is the one who reveals and establishes God's final purpose for his creation. This is telling us that the decisive moment in all of history lies behind us, not ahead of us. Why is this? Because the End was secured—God's final purpose was set in motion—when the Lamb was slain and the Lion triumphed. And now that he has done this, there is nothing that can prevent this great purpose from reaching its glorious completion. This is "what must soon take place" (1:1). Secondly, he is worthy to unseal the scroll because he has "triumphed" (5:5). At the end of each of the seven messages, this word is translated as "victorious" (2:7, 11, 17, 26; 3:5, 12, 21). We have already noted that this raises an obvious question: how do we become victorious? This is where we find our answer, for the Lion is victorious—he has triumphed. And how did he do this? By being the slain Lamb. He triumphed in the cross, by his redeeming death (5:9). We conquer as Jesus did, by self-sacrificing faithfulness. The redeemed are those who "follow the Lamb wherever he goes" (14:3–4), who walk in the way of the cross. Thirdly, if Jesus can put God's great purpose into effect, and if he is the only one who can do so, then no wonder that all of the heavenly beings worship him! And if all of heaven worships him as Savior, Lord, and God, then no one on earth should dare to withhold that worship. So I need to ask: have you added your voice yet to that of the heavenly chorus?

The Scroll and the Seals

The Lamb now begins breaking the seven seals which keep the scroll rolled up. The scroll can't be opened until all seven seals have been broken—like a rolled-up newspaper with seven elastic bands around it. So we do not get to find out what is written on the scroll until after the seventh seal is removed. This tells us something important about what John sees in chapter 6. This sequence of events is not what is on the scroll—it is not so much the content of God's final purpose as the context in which that purpose is accomplished.

The breaking of the first four seals reveals the "four horsemen of the apocalypse" (6:1–8). These introduce the conditions under which most people throughout history—and most today—have lived their lives: military conquest (6:2), social anarchy and violence (6:4), economic division, with hardship for most and luxury for some (6:6), and tragic death (6:8). With the fifth seal John gets to see those who have been martyred for their loyalty to the gospel (6:9–11). In our own time, their number is perhaps greater than it has ever been at any other time in history. They ask how long it will be before God judges the world (6:10)—and that is what John gets to see when the sixth seal is broken (6:12–17). First, he sees the cataclysmic end of this world (6:12–14). Then he sees people of every class and status recoiling in horror from the prospect of facing God (6:15–16). What he is seeing and hearing depicts Judgment Day, the great day of wrath (6:17). The fact is that if God is what the Bible says he is (4:8!), and if I am what the Bible says I am, then it will be terrifying to stand before him. So the final question in chapter 6—"Who can stand?" (6:17)—is exactly the right one to ask—and we desperately need an answer. When we stop and think about what we find in 6:12–17, it becomes clear that we need the answer to another question as well: since we have already reached the End, the last Day, why does Revelation keep going for another sixteen chapters? What else needs to be revealed?

There is now a long interval—all of chapter 7—before the seventh and last seal is broken (8:1). So we won't get to find out what is written on the scroll until chapter 8 at the earliest. What happens in this interval? First, John sees (7:1–2a); then he hears (7:2b–8); again he sees (7:9–12); and finally he hears once more (7:13–17). The first two of these go together, as they deal with the sealing of God's servants, while the next two focus on an uncountable multitude before the throne. What does all of this tell us?

John sees four angels who have the power to harm the world. They are restrained until God's servants are "sealed." There are three questions we need to ask about this. The first is what "sealing" means. In that world, the seal was a mark of ownership. When God's servants are sealed, they are identified as his and thus placed under his protection. So they will be secure even when "harm" arrives (7:2–3). How does God do this sealing? Not literally by marking our foreheads, of course, but by giving us his Spirit when we believe the gospel (2 Cor 1:21–22; Eph 1:13–14; 4:30). This confirms something we learned as we were investigating chapter 1: that is, John's visions draw on imagery used in the apostles' teaching.

Secondly, when does this sealing take place? John doesn't see it, but only hears about it (7:4). Yet it is obvious that 7:1–8 concerns things that happen before Judgment Day (6:12–17). What John hears about here happens at the beginning of the salvation-story for each believer: we are sealed by the Holy Spirit when we first put our trust in the Lord Jesus. So 7:1–8 is about something that takes place well before what we find in 6:12–17. This alerts us to the fact that the visions in Revelation are not necessarily in chronological order. As we will discover in the following chapters, this is not the only place where there are flashbacks. Calendarizers take note! It is not possible to read off a calendar of the future in the book of Revelation.

Thirdly, who are the servants who are sealed? It comes as something of a disappointment to learn that there are only 144,000 of them—and that they are all Jewish! This implies that most of us will miss out. Yet this is not what it seems. We are told that the 144,000 come from "all the tribes of Israel" (7:4). But the list that follows contains two "mistakes": the tribe of Dan is missing, and Joseph is there twice (as Joseph and as Manasseh, one of his sons). John and many of the members of his churches would have noticed these errors immediately—so why are they there? Could it be a signal that we are not meant to take this literally? There are several reasons for reaching this conclusion. The first is the number itself, which appears to be a symbol for the totality of God's people. Twelve is the number which stands for the people of God (see 21:12–14), and 12,000 speaks of the perfection of the city of God (21:15–16), which represents his people (21:9–10). Secondly, John only hears about the 144,000 servants of God (7:3–8). What he actually sees is an uncountable multitude of God's servants from every nation, tribe, people, and language-group (7:9, 15). What is the connection between these two groups? The most likely answer is that they are one and the same: the multitude John sees is the 144,000 he has just heard about—just as the slain Lamb he saw is the triumphant Lion he was told about (5:5–6).

So what exactly does John see? It is as though another tier has been added to the grandstand that he saw in 5:8–13, for now he sees a countless multitude of people joining in the praise of God and the Lamb (7:9–10). What they are saying is endorsed and amplified by the angelic host (7:11–12). This vast assembly is doing what the frantic people at the end of the previous chapter assumed could not happen (6:17). They are standing before the throne and the Lamb (7:9)—and they are not terrified by his wrath! On the contrary, they are rejoicing in his salvation (7:10). How are we to explain the total contrast between these two groups? Why does the sight of God's face strike some with terror and fill others with joy? Is there an answer in what we read next?

When he sees this throng and their worship, John is asked who they are (7:13). His discreet response leads to a detailed answer to this question (7:14–17). This tells us four important things about the people John sees. First, they have come out of what is called "the great tribulation" (v.14). The word that is used here also occurs in 1:9 and 2:22, where it is translated as "suffering," and in 2:9, where it is translated as "afflictions." So 7:14 is not Revelation's way of speaking about some terrible ordeal that still lies ahead of us. Instead it is most likely referring to what John has seen as the first five seals were broken from the scroll (6:1–11). He is being told that the people in this vision have gone through all the suffering that life in this world brings to believers, including persecution.

Secondly, they are wearing white robes (7:9, 13–14). This is meant to remind us of what Jesus says to the church in Sardis (3:4–5). There we learn that people dressed in white robes are the victors referred to at the end of each message to the churches. So despite everything that a sinful and hostile world can throw at them, the people in this vast assembly have triumphed. This is not because they are superheroes, but because they are sealed (7:3–4). God really does protect and preserve his servants.

Thirdly, their robes are white because they have washed them in lamb's blood (7:14). If we needed a reminder that Revelation is using picture language rather than speaking literally, then here it is. No amount of washing in blood would ever turn a garment white! The reference to the blood of the Lamb is meant to send us back to 1:5 and 5:9. Taken together, these three verses are reminding us that we are saved out of sin and judgment into fellowship with God by Jesus' atoning death. By dying for us, he has set us free from sin (1:5), purchased us for God (5:9), and made us clean (7:14). As a result, we can face God confident and not confounded, assured and not afraid. But this peace and joy are only for those who have taken hold of what the Lord Jesus did for us on the cross—who have "washed their robes . . . in the blood of the Lamb" (7:14). (I hope this is true of you.) At the End, every human being will be calling out, either to the mountains and rocks (6:16) or to the Emperor and the Lamb (7:10), either in terror or in grateful, joyful praise.

Fourthly, if the people John is seeing have experienced the "suffering" mentioned in 1:9, they also share in the "kingdom." So they are before God's throne, that is, in the very presence of the King of kings (7:15). As a result, they will enjoy everything that flows from the complete and unchallenged exercise of his sovereign, saving rule. They will be utterly secure because he shelters them (v.15). They will be completely satisfied and content, because they will never experience any deprivation or hardship (v.16). They will be under the shepherding care of the enthroned Lamb, a royal redeemer who will supply them with life that never diminishes (v.17). And God will tenderly remove every trace of their sorrows and griefs (v.17)—and will make sure that they never have any more by getting rid of everything that could cause it (Isa 25:7–8). Second-time readers will know that John is going to find out a lot more about the glorious future that is waiting for God's people—but this brief glimpse is enough to show us how stunningly good life in God's heavenly kingdom is going to be. Why wouldn't you want to have a place in something this good? And you most certainly will have a place in this kingdom if you wash your robes in the blood of the Lamb.

Before we move on to the next section of this book, we need to note the big question raised by what John sees and hears here. I wonder if you saw it—or rather, noticed its absence. Something is missing from this vision—something without which this vast assembly would not have known about the cleansing that comes from Jesus' death (v.14) and would not be praising him for his great salvation (v.10). They must somehow have heard the gospel. That gives us our question: how did the gospel reach people from every nation, tribe, people, and language-group? We will have to read on, looking for an answer—just as we are still waiting for an answer to another important question: what is written on the scroll that the Lamb has taken from the Emperor's right hand?

When we look back over chapters 6 and 7, we learn something important about this book. We have gone from the way life in this world is for most people (6:1–8) to the way it treats many believers (6:9–11) and then on to Judgment Day (6:12–17). What John hears next (7:3–8) happens at the beginning of our salvation-story, when we are sealed by God, while what he sees (7:9–12) happens at the end of that story, when we stand before God. It is obvious, therefore, that John is not being given visions of the history of the world, starting from his own time and then working in chronological order through each part of the story until we reach the End. So one of the things we must try to find out is the reason that his visions seem to go backwards and forwards through time.

That is something we will be looking out for in the next section of the book.

We began this chapter at the door which admitted John into heaven. When he saw it, he was told that he was to be shown "what must take place" in the future (4:1). We now know what lies at the heart of this future. The Day of Judgment will come upon all people, no matter what their class or status (6:15). And all of the redeemed, the entire people of God, will enter into the fulness of final salvation. But now that we have reached the End and seen these final realities, what is left to be seen? Why does Revelation continue for another fifteen chapters?

Questions for Reading 4:1–7:17 Again

1. Why does this second vision begin with a throne?

2. What do chapters 4 and 5 teach us about heavenly reality?

3. What is John seeing in chapter 6?

4. How do the two halves of chapter 7 fit together?

Chapter 3

For All Nations

Revelation 8:1—11:18

OUR READING OF REVELATION 1–7 has given us four questions that need an answer. First, we want to know what is written on the scroll that the Lamb took from the Emperor's hand (5:7). This cannot be unrolled until all seven of its seals have been broken open. And we are just about to reach this point—so we are eagerly waiting for the contents of this important document to be revealed. Our second question concerns the vast multinational, multicultural assembly that John has seen before the throne (7:9). How did they hear the gospel, so that they knew about the cleansing power of the Lamb's blood (7:14) and came to participate in his salvation? Thirdly, why are John's visions not travelling in a straight line through history, but going backwards and forwards between his time and the End? Finally, now that John has seen both Judgment Day (6:12–17) and the final salvation of God's people (7:9–17), what else can be left for him to see? Since we have reached the End, why does he need any more visions? Will we find answers to these questions in this second part of John's second vision?

For most readers of Revelation, the first seven chapters are not too bad, for they give us a reasonable amount that we can understand and use. But from 8:1 onwards, it seems to go downhill quite rapidly, improving only in the last two chapters! From this point on, it feels as though we meet a lot of bizarre and very unpleasant things that are hard to understand and hard to accept. So now is a good time to remind ourselves of what we learned by reading chapter 1. The combination of 1:2 and 1:9 tells us that what John sees is what he already knew. These strange and puzzling visions are not revelations of new truth. John and the churches are not being shown things they didn't know. What John sees is the word of God and the testimony of Jesus Christ (1:2)—so these visions are new ways of presenting truth that was familiar to them. And what truth is this? What John sees in the rest of this second vision is what Jesus taught his disciples when they asked him, "[W]hat will be the sign of your coming and of the end of the age?" (Matt 24:3). He answered as follows:

> Watch out that no one deceives you. For many will come in my name, claiming, 'I am the Messiah,' and will deceive many. You will hear of wars and rumors of wars, but see to it that you are not alarmed. Such things must happen, but the end is still to come. Nation will rise against nation, and kingdom against kingdom. There will be famines and earthquakes in various places. All these are the beginning of birth pains. Then you will be handed over to be persecuted and put to death, and you will be hated by all nations because of me. At that time many will turn away from the faith and will betray and hate each other, and many false prophets will appear and deceive many people. Because of the increase of wickedness, the love of most will grow cold, but the one who stands firm to the end will be saved. And this gospel of the kingdom will be preached in the whole world as a testimony to all nations, and then the end will come. (Matt 24:4–14)

This is what John now gets to see. So let us look at what he tells us about the End and what leads up to it.

Warnings for the Nations

We have reached the point where the Lamb breaks open the seventh seal (8:1)—and what happens then? Nothing! There is no unrolling of the scroll so that its contents can be revealed, nor is there any other activity in the heavenly throne-room. There is just a lengthy silence. This is a dramatic pause that heightens tension and increases expectation. By the time it ended, John would be almost bursting, straining to see what is coming. This turns out to be seven angels, each of whom is given a trumpet (8:2). Then John sees these trumpets being sounded (8:6–11:15). So is this the contents of the scroll? No, this is the contents of the seventh seal. The breaking of the first six seals introduces activity that John sees and hears (6:1–17), and the breaking of the last seal does the same. Like the first six, this too reveals more about the context in which the Emperor's purpose and will is worked out. John is about to see what happens when each of the trumpets is sounded—and only then will the contents of the scroll be revealed. There is such a long delay before this finally happens that what the scroll contains must be momentous indeed. But we will have to wait before we find out what that is.

So what happens when the trumpets are sounded? The first thing to note is that what John now sees and hears follows the same pattern as the seven seals: the first four belong together and are described briefly, the fifth and sixth introduce activity that is described at greater length, and then there is a lengthy interval before the seventh one. When the first four trumpets are sounded (8:7–12), disasters strike four basic aspects of the natural world: the land, the sea, fresh water, and the planets. In each case, the damage they inflict is limited to one-third. And like everything else in the book so far, what John sees is pictorial and not literal. This is obvious when we get to 8:12. If a third of the sun was destroyed, we would not lose sunlight for a third of the day, but all of the daylight would be only two-thirds of its normal brightness. This would have been just as obvious to John and the churches as it is to us, so they would have known not to take these pictures literally. The fifth trumpet introduces an invasion of immense locusts (9:1–11) that wound like scorpions (9:3, 5, 10) and look like horses (9:7). Again, the harm they do is limited: they torture but do not kill (9:5), and they do so for only five months (9:5, 10). The sixth trumpet introduces a vast cavalry assault (9:13–21), with horses that partially resemble lions (9:17) and snakes (9:19). This brings about the deaths of one-third of humankind (9:15, 18). Then there is a long interval (10:1–11:14) before the last trumpet is sounded (11:15).

We will direct our attention to the first six trumpets (8:7–9:21) before we look at the long interval in 10:1–11:14. There are three questions we need to ask about this part of John's vision. First, what is John seeing? With the first four trumpets (8:7–12), we have a vivid and dramatic portrayal of natural disasters. It reminds us of Jesus' words: "There will be great earthquakes, famines and pestilences in various places, and fearful events and great signs from heaven." (Luke 21:11).

What about the events of chapter 9? The locusts John saw came from the Abyss (9:2–3), and had the angel of the Abyss as their king (9:11). Second-time readers will know that the Abyss is connected with Satan (11:7; 17:8; 20:1–3; cf. Luke 8:30–31). And the locusts' king is called the Destroyer (which is what the Hebrew and Greek names in 9:11 mean). This is obviously a way of referring to the devil. So the locusts John sees are what Paul calls "the powers of this dark world and . . . the spiritual forces of evil in the heavenly realms" (Eph 6:12). This is a vision of supernatural evil—but this is directed not at believers but only at those who are not God's servants (9:4; cf. 7:3).

What about the cavalry introduced by the sixth trumpet? The events of the fifth trumpet would have reminded those who knew their Bibles of the description of a locust plague in Joel 1–2. This part of the Old Testament also contains many similarities to the events of the sixth trumpet. The invading locusts are said to be a vast army (Joel 1:6; 2:2, 5, 7, 11, 25). More particularly, they are compared to cavalry (Joel 2:4). They are also said to be like lions (Joel 1:6), and their impact is like that of a fire (Joel 1:19–20; 2:3,

5). We should also note the two calls to sound the trumpet (Joel 2:1, 15). All of this suggests that the events of the sixth trumpet are simply another way of seeing those of the fifth trumpet. Here too John is seeing the forces of evil. This is confirmed by the way fire, smoke, and sulfur (9:17–18) are later shown to be connected with the devil (14:10–11; 19:20; 20:10; 21:8). And here too this is directed against unbelievers (9:20–21). So the fifth and sixth trumpets introduce complementary depictions of the powers of darkness in their ferocity against all human beings who do not belong to the Lord Jesus.

Now to the second question we need to ask about what John is seeing here: when do these things happen? Since the sixth seal introduced Judgment Day (6:12–17), what John gets to see here must happen before that. When we get to Judgment Day, we have reached the End! This confirms something we have already learned about Revelation: that is, the sequence in which John sees things is not the same as the order in which they happen. His visions do not line up one after the other. We are now in a position to work out why that is. We can think of what he tells us as like the printing of a color magazine. The printing-press passes over the paper to lay down one color, and then it returns to the beginning and passes over the paper again, this time laying down a different color. The final picture is built up one color at a time. So it is with John's visions. We get to the End (6:12–17; 7:9–17), only to go back to the beginning and start again . . . and then again . . . and again. Why is it like this? The reason is that our world and our history are complex—they have many dimensions and layers, and so cannot easily be depicted in one vision. The first five seals introduced one aspect of our world: evils of human origin. The trumpets introduce another two aspects: natural disasters and supernatural evil. While John sees them in sequence, they occur simultaneously. And all three are in effect throughout human history; they do not occur only at the End.

This now enables us to answer another of the questions we noted at the beginning of this chapter. By the end of chapter 7, John has seen the End from both sides: final judgment (6:12–17) and final salvation (7:9–17). So what else is left for him to see? What we have now discovered points us to this answer: if we see the End too soon, we will not appreciate it fully, as we will not have a big enough view of what it brings to an end. We need to see life in this world from several angles before we can see why the End needs to be what it is.

And so to the third question we should ask about this part of the book: why do these things happen? The fact is that both natural disasters and supernatural evils are part of human experience in this world. Yet God is on the throne: he rules as the Lord God Almighty (4:2, 8). All things are under his control and serve his purpose—so what role can these things play in the purposes of God? Our passage gives us four clues which point us to the answer. I wonder if you noticed them as you read these chapters. The first and most obvious is in 9:20. By telling us that those who were spared in the plagues "still did not repent," John is making it clear that these events should have brought people to repentance. Getting people to turn away from self-reliant rejection of God and to turn to him is an important part of their function. The second clue is John's use of the word "plagues" (9:18, 20). This alerts us to the fact that what John is seeing resembles the plagues in Egypt. The events of the first trumpet make us think of Exodus 9:23–26; those of the second trumpet, Exodus 7:20–21; those of the fourth trumpet, Exodus 10:21–23; and those of the fifth trumpet, Exodus 10:12–15. Why did God send these plagues upon Egypt? They were warnings, intended to bring the Pharaoh to repentance. They were also judgments upon his hard-hearted refusal to repent (Exod 7:13, 22; 8:15, 19, 32; 9:7, 34–35). So the plagues, too, were intended to put repentance on the agenda. The third clue is the parallels we have noted between 9:1–19 and Joel 1–2. We learn from Joel that the destructive invasion of locusts was meant to cause Israel to return to the Lord (Joel 2:12–13). That is, it was meant to bring them to repentance (Joel 1:8, 13–14; 2:15–17). The fourth and final clue is the fact that these events are introduced by the sounding of trumpets. One of the functions this has in the Bible is that it warns of approaching danger: it gives the alarm (Jer 6:17; Ezek 33:1–6;

Joel 2:1). What these four clues tell us is that both natural disasters and supernatural evils are used by God to sound an alarm, to warn people of danger, to call them to repentance. Before God brings final judgment, he warns us again and again through preliminary judgments. He did this repeatedly in the history of Israel:

> Are my ways unjust, people of Israel? Is it not your ways that are unjust? . . . Repent! Turn away from all your offences; then sin will not be your downfall . . . Why will you die, people of Israel? For I take no pleasure in the death of anyone, declares the Sovereign LORD. Repent and live! (Ezek 18:29–32)

And he is still doing so, as Jesus told his hearers (Luke 13:1–9). God shakes everything to point us to the only unshakeable reality: his eternal kingdom (Heb 12:25–28). He unsettles us, disturbing our stability so that we will flee to him and rely only on him.

John now gets to see another mighty angel (10:1; cf. 5:2). His lion-like roar triggers off seven thunders (10:3), but John is not allowed to record what these thunders said (10:4). This is a reminder that Revelation does not reveal everything about God and his purposes: God still has his secrets (Deut 29:29). It is what the angel has to say that matters—and his announcement is what we have been waiting for! John now learns that the sounding of the seventh trumpet will mean that God's "mystery" is accomplished (10:7). This mystery is God's secret purpose, what he intends to do (see Dan 2:27–28, 44–45). This is, in other words, what is written on the Emperor's scroll. As we have been expecting, when the seventh seal was broken the scroll could be unrolled and its contents revealed. That is what is just about to happen. The angel says that God has disclosed this secret to the prophets (note Dan 2:29–30, 44–47). This means that an important part of the prophets' role was to announce in advance what God is going to do at the End. Do you see what this tells us? It means that there is a sense in which we already know what is written on the scroll, even before it is opened. That is because the prophets have told us about God's End-time purpose. What they have revealed still has a mysterious side to it, as they weren't allowed to know everything (1 Pet

1:10–11). Yet at least the big picture is clear. What that is we are just about to find out.

Witness to the Nations

But before the seventh trumpet is sounded (11:15), John gets to see and hear several other things. Because he deals with them so briefly, we are going to pass over what is recorded in 10:8–11 and 11:1–2 in order to focus our attention on 11:3–14. This faces us with an obvious question: who are these two witnesses? John gives us six clues that point us to the answer. Did you see them on your way through the passage? The first is the fact that they are "witnesses" (11:3) who give "their testimony" (11:7). This means that they are like John, for he does what a witness does: that is, he "testifies" (1:2). They are also like Jesus, the "faithful witness" (1:5; 3:14), for he too "testifies" (22:20). And they are like Antipas, who was a "faithful witness" even to the point of death (2:13). Finally, they are like those martyred for their witness, "the testimony they had maintained" (6:9; 12:11). These witnesses are all bearers of the gospel.

Secondly, they are said to be "the two lampstands that stand before the Lord of the earth" (11:4). This points us back to 1:12, 20, where we find that the lampstands in John's first vision represent the churches.

Thirdly, we are told that "fire comes from their mouths and devours their enemies" (11:5). We know that this will be no more literal than the rest of John's visions. So their enemy gets near enough to kill them without even being slightly singed (11:7)! And when Jesus' disciples had a similar fate in mind for people in a Samaritan village, he rebuked them (Luke 9:51–55). What John is seeing here is another mobile metaphor. The fire represents God's word (Jer 20:9; 23:29)—especially the word of judgment that the prophet speaks against hardhearted rebels (Jer 5:14).

Fourthly, they have twin powers to do harm (11:6). The first is that they can prevent the rain. This is a reminder of what happened during the ministry of the prophet Elijah (1 Kgs 17:1, 7;

18:1, 41–45). Their second power is to turn the waters into blood and to strike the earth with every kind of plague—an obvious reference to Moses and the plagues in Egypt (Exod 7:14–21; 11:1). As the greatest of them, Moses and Elijah represent God's prophets (Matt 17:3)—and this is what the witnesses are (11:3, 10). They have tormented "those who live on the earth" (11:10), which in Revelation is a way of referring to unbelievers (3:10; 6:10; 13:8, 14; 14:6–7; 17:2, 8). How have they been tormented by the witnesses? The passage implies that it was their testimony, their prophesying, that caused this distress. This reminds us of what the apostle Paul tells us: that for unbelievers, those who proclaim the gospel can be as unwelcome as the stench of death (2 Cor 2:14–16).

Fifthly, they are killed in "the great city" (11:8). Second-time readers will know that this is later to be called Babylon (16:19). But here we are told that it is Sodom, Egypt, and Jerusalem ("where also their Lord was crucified"). And its citizens are "the inhabitants of the earth" (11:9–10): that is, unbelievers. In the Bible, Babylon represents the ruthless use of power and wealth against God's people (17:5–6; 18:5, 10, 13–17, 24); Sodom represents gross immorality, the rejection of God's law (Jude 7); Egypt speaks of persecution, the rejection of God's people; and Jerusalem points to rebellion, the rejection of God's covenant—and of his Son. Put all this together, and this great city represents what Jesus calls "the world": that is, unbelieving humankind in rebellion against God (Matt 18:6–7; Luke 16:8; John 7:7; 12:31; 16:8–11; 17:9, 14, 16, 25).

Sixthly, the witnesses come to life and ascend to heaven in a cloud (11:11–12). This is obviously meant to remind us of the Lord Jesus himself, resurrected out of death and exalted to heavenly glory (Acts 1:1–11).

Where do we get to when we put all of these clues together? They tell us that *we* are the two witnesses. So John is seeing what Jesus said about the mission of his church: "this gospel of the kingdom will be preached in the whole world as a testimony to all nations . . . go and make disciples of all nations . . ." (Matt 24:14; 28:19). He is also seeing something else that Jesus taught his disciples: "If the world hates you, keep in mind that it hated me first . . . If they persecuted me, they will persecute you also." (John 15:18, 20). But why are there two witnesses? If they represent God's church, wouldn't one be enough? This is likely to reflect the biblical principle that at least two witnesses are required for their testimony to be considered valid (Num 35:30; Deut 17:6; 19:15; Matt 18:16; John 8:17; 2 Cor 13:1; 1 Tim 5:19; Heb 10:28). Because it comes from two witnesses, the world has no excuse for not heeding this testimony.

Now we have our answer to another of the questions we carried over from the previous chapter. There are people from every nation, tribe, people, and language-group standing in the presence of God at the End (7:9–10) because in fulfillment of Jesus' prophecy (Matt 24:14) and in obedience to his command (Matt 28:19–20), God's people have carried the gospel to the ends of the world. The inhabitants of the earth have heard the gospel from the two witnesses.

We have now almost reached the end of John's second vision. But before we look at how it ends, it will be helpful to think about what he has seen in the second half of this vision. We have discovered that God has two ways of speaking to the world: by trumpets (8:6–9:21) and by testimony (11:3–12). He calls out to us in his warnings. That is, all the upheavals and hardships of this life are used by God to call us away from relying on anything that can be shaken—from false hopes, false securities, false gods. And he also calls out through his witnesses: those who hold out the gospel to every nation, calling all peoples to repentance. By calling out to us in these quite different ways, God is being merciful to the world before final judgment comes.

King of the Nations

And now we come to the moment we have been waiting for. Ever since the Lamb took the scroll from the Emperor's right hand (5:7), we have been waiting to discover what is written on it. At last the seventh trumpet is sounded (11:15). This means that the contents of the Emperor's scroll can finally be revealed. To say the same thing in another way, it means that God's mystery will now be accomplished (10:7). So what has the Emperor decreed? What is the secret purpose which God has announced in advance to the prophets? What is so essential for us to know that John wept when he thought it would not be disclosed (5:4)? Here it is: "The kingdom of this world has become the kingdom of our Lord and of his Messiah, and he will reign for ever and ever." (11:15).

That's it? But we already knew about this. Exactly! That is because what John is seeing is not something new but something well-known—the word of God and the testimony of Jesus Christ (1:2). But what makes this announcement so important that we have had to wait six chapters for it? We get some idea by looking at the way the elders rejoice when the announcement is made. What they say makes it clear that something new and wonderful has now arrived: the Lord God Almighty has begun to reign (11:17). In one sense, this has always been true: God's throne is the center of all heavenly reality, and his reign is eternal (4:2, 9–10). In another sense, this came about when the Lord Jesus won the decisive victory in his death and resurrection and began his heavenly reign as King of kings (3:21; 17:14; 19:16). Those who belong to him participate in this kingdom here and now (1:6, 9). But what has just been announced at the sounding of the seventh trumpet is even greater than this. Throughout history, God has allowed the world to challenge his authority and exercise limited but real power over us—but that kingdom is now at an end. We have now reached the climax of the story, when God begins to rule in a way that is complete and unchallenged, expressing his majesty as God without holding back in any way. This comprehensive exercise of his sovereign rule is so much greater than what came before that it is as though God has only just "begun to reign" (11:17). This changes everything. John has been seeing the ways in which life in this world is chaotic, harsh, and threatening—but this will not last. Not only natural disasters but also human evil and spiritual evil will not go on forever. The world as we know it is destined to come to an end when the kingdom of our Lord God and his Messiah is fully and finally established. When his sovereign power is exercised in this unlimited way in every part of his creation, this world will be totally transformed. The coming kingdom of God means nothing less than a new world: by taking his great power and beginning his reign, God makes everything new (11:17; 21:5).

This kingdom of God means final salvation and final judgment (11:18). Since the Lord who rules is the "the God of all grace" (1 Pet 5:10), his End-time kingdom will mean the complete and unlimited expression of his saving grace. So all of his people—every one without exception, even the very least and lowest—will receive their reward, sharing in all the riches of his great salvation. But the God who rules is also utterly and intensely holy (4:8), a consuming fire (Heb 12:29). His End-time kingdom will therefore mean the complete and unlimited expression of the blazing purity of his holiness. Those who have denied God the honor that belongs to him by worshiping false gods and who have defied his will (9:20–21) will go down into judgment, for they are destroyers like the one to whom they belong (11:18; cf. 9:11). Hence the trumpets (8:6–9:21): God warns the peoples of the world through preliminary judgments which are intended to call us away from what will lead to final judgment. It is also why he sends his witnesses, announcing his kingdom and calling the nations to repentance.

By ending in this way, what John sees and hears in this second half of his second vision has some important reminders for us. First, through all the chaos of life in this world and all the ways in which it can hurt us, God is working out his final purpose. Nothing can prevent him from bringing in the End that he has appointed, the glories of full and final salvation in his eternal kingdom. And this means that in all things—no matter how evil or how destructive—he is at work for the good of those who love him, who have been called according to his purpose (Rom 8:28). He will most certainly bring us through "the great tribulation" of this life (7:14) to stand before his throne, rejoicing in his great salvation (7:9–10, 15–17).

Secondly, the gospel that we are to take to all the nations of the world announces this End-time kingdom. It proclaims that the End has already begun at Easter, and so cannot fail to come in its fulness when the redeeming, risen, reigning Jesus returns. It calls upon all peoples everywhere to repent (Matt 4:17; Luke 24:47; Acts 17:30–31), in view of the fact that his kingdom has come already and is coming still.

We began this chapter with four questions, and we have found answers for three of them. We now know what is written on the Emperor's scroll (5:1–7): it announces his purpose to set up his everlasting kingdom. We also know how the vast multitude of the redeemed (7:9–17) heard the gospel: it reaches all the peoples of the world through the witness of God's church. And the reason John's visions do not take us through history in a straight line is that the complex reality of life in this world needs to be looked at from a number of different angles. Although John gets to see these one after the other, they are all true at the same time. But now that we have reached the End again, what more needs to be revealed? What haven't we seen yet? Why does Revelation keep going for another eleven chapters?

Questions for Reading 8:1–11:18 Again

1. When do we get to find out what is written on the Emperor's scroll? How do we know when its contents are revealed?

2. What do the trumpets reveal?

3. How do we work out who the two witnesses are?

4. By the time we get to 11:15, what do we know about the "kingdom of the world"?

Chapter 4

The War of the Trinities
Revelation 11:19—15:4

WE HAVE REACHED THE End—and yet we are only half-way through Revelation. But now that the End has been announced (11:15–18), surely all that remains is for John to see it. So why does the book continue for another eleven chapters? What else does John need to see? What appears now is the opened temple (11:19), and then a dazzling queen about to give birth (12:1–2), an enormous dragon with an appetite for young royal flesh (12:3–4), a war in heaven (12:7–12), and a hot pursuit on earth (12:13–17). What is going on here? What is John seeing in this chapter—and why does he need to see it?

Because it is so easy to lose our way when we are reading this unfamiliar book, it will help us to start by reminding ourselves of some important things we have learned about it. We know that John is seeing gospel truth: "the word of God and the testimony of Jesus Christ" (1:2). We also know that the order in which he sees things is not always the order in which they happen. The printing-press had completed its first run by the end of chapter 7, for by then we had seen both final judgment (6:12–17) and final salvation (7:9–17). Now it has done another run across the page, bringing us to the End again (11:15–18). This means that we have seen the complex reality of life in this world from four angles: evils of human origin (6:1–11), natural disasters (8:7–12), supernatural evil (9:1–21), and universal Christian witness (11:3–12). Are we now seeing another run of the press, laying down another color? That is, are we being shown other dimensions of human experience? Let's take a closer look at what John sees and hears in this section.

This vision, like the next one (15:5), begins with the temple being opened (11:19). What is this telling us? It is actually very important and somewhat surprising news. One of the major functions of the Temple was to remind God's people that he is present with them (Exod 25:8–9; 29:44–46; 1 Kgs 6:11–13). But since he is a holy God, access to him had to be carefully controlled. So the temple was set up as a series of barriers which progressively excluded more and more people. The final barrier excluded absolutely everyone except the high priest—and even he was permitted through this barrier (a huge curtain) only once each year (Lev 16). What this curtain shielded from view was the ark of the covenant (Exod 26:31–34; 40:1–3; 1 Kgs 8:6–10). This covenant-box was also the footstool of God's symbolic throne (2 Sam 6:2; Pss 99:1, 5; 132:7–8). It was thus a reminder that he is a great King who rules his people and the world. But now the temple has been opened right up: the curtain has gone (Mark 15:38), and John can see the ark of the covenant. This is a vivid, pictorial way of making the same point as Hebrews 10:19–22: because of Jesus and his death, there is now no barrier to keep us from God. We can come freely to him and have real fellowship with him. He is a God of amazing grace--but this has not in any way diminished his awesome greatness. So as soon as the temple is opened, there is lightning, thunder, a hail-storm, and an earthquake. This takes us back to John's vision of the throne (4:5), and then back to Mount Sinai (Exod 19:16; Heb 12:18–21). It reminds us that the covenant-making, covenant-keeping King is a God of immense power and intense holiness. It renews the "heavenly perspective" of chapter 4, before John has to see some very disturbing sights. It is God's way of telling the churches to remember the throne (4:2). It says, "Don't lose your bearings in what is just about to happen. No matter what you hear, no matter how terrible it is, don't forget that God reigns. He is the Lord, and his reign is a reign of grace and power. And if this God is for us, who can be against us?"

The Mother and the Dragon

Between his two glimpses of the opened temple (11:91; 15:5), John sees two great signs (12:1; 15:1). The first of these turns out to be a double sign (12:1, 3), and chapters 12 to 14 focus on this twin sign and its outcomes. So what is John seeing here? There are three fixed points which help us work it out. Did you notice them as you read chapter 12? The first is in 12:5. This tells us that the male child who is born to the queen "will rule all the nations with an iron scepter." In 2:27, Jesus applies these words of Psalm 2:9 to the authority he has been given by the Father. We are also told in 12:5 that this child is "snatched up to God and to his throne." This is meant to remind us of Jesus' exaltation to heaven (Acts 1:9–11). It takes us back to 3:21, where Jesus says that his victory now means sitting with the Father on his throne. It also takes us back to 5:6, where we learn that the Messiah, the Lion-Lamb, shares God's throne. The second fixed point is in 12:9, where we learn that the dragon (12:3) is Satan. The third is in 12:17, which indicates that the other children of the queen are Christian believers.

With these fixed points to guide us, we can interpret what John sees in chapter 12. It is depicting the fact that the coming of Jesus brings the age-old conflict with Satan to a climax. Satan attempted to destroy him (12:4), but Jesus defeated him, as his resurrection and exaltation to heaven showed (12:5b). Enraged by his defeat, Satan is now seeking to destroy God's people (12:17). In chapter 9, we had a vision of supernatural evil directed against unbelievers (9:4, 20–21). Now the focus changes, and it is believers who are in the firing-line.

What about the war between Michael and the dragon (12:7–12)? What does this mean? And why is it Michael and not Jesus who defeats the devil? Here is another place where we need to notice exactly what John is telling us. He begins by describing what he sees (12:7–9), and then he tells us what he hears (12:10–12). As usual, what he hears gives us the meaning of what he has seen. The heavenly voice begins by announcing the arrival of God's kingdom: "Now have come the salvation and the power and the kingdom of our God, and the authority of his Messiah" (12:10a). This is not the same event as that celebrated in 11:15. That was the final coming of the kingdom, its completion; this is its first coming, its commencement. That is the End; this is Easter. That will mean the destruction of the devil (19:19–20; 20:10), while here he is defeated but still active (12:12). There is a direct connection between these two, for the End begins at Easter. And what does Easter mean? It is the time of the great triumph, the decisive victory in the war between God and Satan. As victory-time, Easter is the time of the Lamb and the Lion—it is when the Lamb sheds his blood (12:11), and when the Lion-Messiah enters upon his heavenly authority (12:10). So it is through Jesus' death (the Lamb) and resurrection-exaltation (the Lion) that Satan is defeated—he is "hurled down" (12:9, 10b; cf. 12:13) and is on his way to his final overthrow.

What is Michael's role in all of this? He is not the Victor. Rather, in his role as protector of God's people (Dan 12:1), he acts on behalf of the Messiah. What John sees him doing is applying the victory and thus establishing the salvation won by the Lamb-Lion. The power he displays and the authority he exercises belong to God and his Messiah (12:10a). This victory brings "salvation" to God's people (12:10a). The endless accusations of the defeated Accuser fall on deaf ears (12:10b): there is now no condemnation for those who are in Christ Jesus (Rom 8:1). So what John sees and hears here is what Paul affirms in Romans 8:33–34, for example.

And God's people are seen here as victors: "they triumphed over him" (12:11) uses the word that is translated as "victorious" in the letters to the seven churches. So here is another answer to the question raised but not answered by those seven messages (2:1–3:22): that is, how do you win the victory? The victory in view at this point is over the devil (12:11), and it has twin strands. It comes about "by the blood of the Lamb": that is, Satan's hold on our lives is broken when we trust in Jesus and his death for our sins. It also comes about "by the word of their testimony": that is, Satan's designs on other people's lives are thwarted when we bear our testimony to Jesus and the gospel. The full extent of this victory is measured by our attitude to life and death (12:11b). Those who belong to Jesus see their own lives in the light of his death. This shows us that it is better to remain faithful even if it costs us our life than to save our life by becoming unfaithful (see 2:10; 6:9; 14:12–13). When his ultimate sanction, the threat of death, no longer has any hold over us, then Satan's reign is truly at an end (Heb 2:14–15). Even in the face of death, God's blood-ransomed people keep holding fast to the cross and keep holding out the gospel.

Who is the queen who features in all of this action? In 12:5, she seems to be Jesus' mother, Mary. Yet she flies on eagle's wings to the wilderness, where God cares for her (12:6, 14). This makes her sound like Israel (Exod 19:4; Deut 1:30–31; 2:7; 32:10–11). Then in 12:17 she appears to represent the church. How can she be all of these at the same time? Here we discover another important characteristic of these visions. Some of the pictures John is seeing are rather like the political cartoons which feature characters such as "Uncle Sam." This top-hatted, bearded figure with the stars-and-stripes waistcoat can represent the American President, the American government, the American people, or the American way-of-life. The particular cartoon in which he appears will enable us to work out which of these the cartoonist has in mind on this occasion. In some cases, Uncle Sam might represent more than one or even all of these. In a similar way, this royal lady stands for the faithful, persecuted people of God, seen from several different angles.

The Mock Trinity

Chapter 12 ends on an ominous note, with the frustrated and enraged dragon setting off to wage war against believers. Chapter 13 reveals how he does this. It turns out that the dragon has two allies, one a beast that comes out of the sea (13:1–10) and the other a beast that comes out of the earth (13:11–18). When we read how

John describes the two beasts, it becomes clear that the dragon and his allies represent an evil parody of the triune God, Father, Son, and Spirit.

The beast from the sea is a parody of the Lord Jesus: a false Messiah. The dragon gives him "his power and his throne and great authority" (13:2; cf. 13:4)—just as Jesus receives authority from the Father (2:27; 12:10) and shares his throne (3:21; 5:6). He has a fatal wound that has been healed (13:3)—just as the Lamb is alive although he bears the marks of slaughter (5:6). He is worshiped by people from every tribe, people, language, and nation (13:3, 7–8)—just as those from every nation, tribe, people, and language honor God and the Lamb (7:9–10). His followers bear his mark or name (13:16–17)—just as those who belong to Jesus bear his name (3:12) and his seal (7:3).

The beast from the land is, from one perspective, a parody of the Holy Spirit. He secures people's worship for the sea beast (13:12)—just as the Spirit glorifies the Son (John 16:14) and leads us to worship him as Lord (1 Cor 12:3). He performs signs and wonders (13:13–14)—just as the Spirit works signs to accompany the proclamation of the gospel (Rom 15:19; Heb 2:3–4). He marks the sea beast's followers (13:16–17)—just as the Spirit seals those who believe the gospel (2 Cor 1:21–22; Eph 1:13; 4:30). From another perspective, this beast is the false prophet (16:13). He resembles a lamb but sounds like a dragon (13:11)—just as Jesus warned against false prophets who appear docile (sheep) but are really deadly (wolves).

What John is seeing, therefore, is a fake deity—a deceptive alternative to the true God: a rival object of worship, a rival source of power and authority. This is what the Bible calls an "idol" (1 John 5:20–21). From another angle, it is what Jesus warned his disciples about:

> Watch out that no one deceives you. Many will come in my name, claiming, 'I am he,' and will deceive many . . . For false messiahs and false prophets will appear and perform signs and wonders to deceive, if possible, even the

elect. So be on your guard; I have told you everything ahead of time. (Mark 13:5-6, 22-23).

When does all of this happen? The beginning of this "war against God's holy people" (13:7) seems to coincide with several other events John sees. These are Jesus' exaltation to the throne (12:5) and the defeat of Satan (12:7-12). This war thus begins with the gospel events—with Jesus' salvation-securing death and resurrection.

How long does this war against God's people last? We are given two kinds of answer. The first is three numerical intervals: in 12:6, it is 1260 days; in 12:14, it is "a time, times and half a time" (which comes from Daniel 7:25 and 12:7, and means three and a half years); and in 13:5, it is forty-two months. If each month is taken to be thirty days, these are simply three ways of stating the same period. We have already met this time-span in 11:3, where it is the length of time that the church bears its witness to the world. So this war lasts from Jesus' death and resurrection until his return, from Easter to the End. This confirmed by the second answer, which takes the form of a parallel between what John sees and the story of Israel. God cared for Israel in the wilderness (12:14) after he had rescued them from Egypt and before he led them into the promised land. In the wilderness their redemption was behind them and their inheritance was ahead of them (Exod 15:13, 17; Deut 24:4, 18)—just as, in Christ, we live between redemption and inheritance (Col 1:12-14), between the time when salvation is established and the time when it is completed. So this war on God's people lasts from the day when the kingdom came (12:10) until the day when the kingdom comes (11:15). From one perspective, this period is the time of the church's witness (11:3-12); from another perspective, it is the time of the church's war (12:17; 13:7).

The New Testament has two things to say about this opposition to God and his people. It teaches us that false messiahs and false prophets will be active throughout this entire period—see especially 1 John 2:18, 22-23; 4:1-3 and 2 John 7. It also makes it clear that this will happen with special intensity just before the End (2 Thess 2:1-12).

How is this going to happen? That is, how does the devil make war on God's people? What we see in chapters 12 and 13 presents in pictorial form what we learned in chapters 2 and 3. There we discovered that Satan's attacks on the churches involve a combination of fraud and force, error and terror. Here we see that his war against believers uses the same combination of trickery and tyranny. So there is deception: the land beast fools the earth's inhabitants with great signs and wonders (13:13–14), and the dragon and his allies promote false religion (13:3b–4). And there is oppression: this beast also uses coercive tactics (13:15–17), while the sea beast exercises authority in arrogant and abusive ways (13:5-6). So sometimes Satan's strategy is to mimic God's truth and power; sometimes it is to mock and reject them. We see his war on God's people in such things as the following: the repressive policies of totalitarian governments, whether of the left or the right, which imprison, torture, and kill believers; fanatical religious opponents who persecute and kill Christians; seductive cults and "isms"; shapers of popular opinion who mock the truth and make sin attractive; and charming and plausible heretics who hold important positions in the church.

The Great Divide

The End-time kingdom of God has been announced (11:15)—but we could not see the End yet, before we had seen everything that it must bring to an end. So in this first half of his third vision (12:1–13:18), John sees a tableau of satanic evil. God unmasks Satan here, stripping away the charming, apparently harmless exterior that cloaks his deceptions, in order to reveal the monstrous evil that lies hidden underneath—and probing beneath the hostile exterior of fanatical opponents to reveal the energy that fuels their hatred. All of this raises a rather pressing question: how will we survive such fierce, devious, and unremitting attacks? We find the answer in what John sees next: the Lamb and his followers (14:1–5), three angels making announcements (14:6–13), a double harvest (14:14–20), and a second great sign (15:1–4). The first and last of these belong together, as do the middle two—and each pair makes one fundamental point about the "great divide" between God's people and unbelievers.

God has just revealed the malicious cunning and ruthless brutality of the devil—and now John sees the Lamb and all of God's sealed servants (14:1–5; cf. 7:3–4). This is a reminder that God keeps his people. Despite all the ferocity and duplicity of the devil, God is a great Savior. His people are redeemed (14:3), purchased for God by the Lamb in his death (14:4; cf. 5:9). And they are marked with his name (14:1; cf. 3:12; 7:3), sealed by the Spirit. They also sing the song that only the redeemed know (14:3). This is the song of Moses and the Lamb (15:3)—the song of salvation like the one Moses and Israel sang to celebrate their redemption (Exod 15:1–18); the song of salvation that all who are saved by the Lamb sing (7:9–10, 14). The singers that John sees celebrating God's salvation are the very people who have been assailed by the devil (12:17; 13:7). He may do his worst—but those who are redeemed by the Lamb will share his victory. Part of the "great tribulation" they come through triumphantly (7:14) is the war Satan has waged against them.

The rest of chapter 14 shows us that God's enemies are doomed (14:6–20). This is the point of the three angelic announcements (14:6–11). In God's mercy, there is one last call for everyone to turn to him (14:6–7). Then the fall of Babylon is announced (14:8: see 17:1–18:24), along with judgment on everyone who worships the beast (14:9–11). This is also the point of the two harvests (14:14–20), one of the most common biblical images for judgment. Both of these involve harvesting the earth (14:15–16, 18), indicating the judgment of the whole world. So once more we have reached Judgment Day—the printing press has run over the page again, bringing us to the End as it lays down another color, that is, as it shows us another perspective on life in this world. The Lord Jesus is seen here as the Judge of the world (14:14–16), a divine function he told us he would exercise (see, for example, Matt 25:31–33; John 5:22, 27).

What John sees here (14:1–15:4) makes it very clear that there is a "great divide" at the End—but it begins here and now. There are only two possibilities: to stand on Mount Zion with the Lamb (14:1) or to share in the fall of Babylon (14:8); to bear God's name (14:1) or the mark of the beast (14:9); to sing the new song (14:3) or to drink the cup of wrath (14:10); to follow the Lamb (14:4) or to worship the beast (14:9). John and his churches are being reminded of what they already knew: that there are only two destinies—life or death, salvation or judgment. There is no neutral zone for the agnostics and undecided, because those who have not given their loyalty to the Lamb have effectively rejected him (Matt 12:30; Luke 11:23).

Once more, we have been reminded that in Jesus we share both the suffering and the kingdom (1:9). In this world, we are attacked by the devil—and we are also protected by God. How should we respond to this interplay of peril and preservation, threat and promise? This is where we are directed to the third thing that we share in Jesus: patient endurance (1:9). What he sees here leads John to an important conclusion: "This calls for patient endurance and faithfulness on the part of God's people" (13:10; cf. 14:12). This is how we are to resist the devil as he prowls around like a lion (1 Pet 5:8–9), or as he seeks to pass himself off as an angel of light (2 Cor 11:14). We must resolve to be loyal in the face of both error and terror—to refuse to give in to trickery or to give up under tyranny. In view of all that John has seen in his third vision, now is a fitting time to set myself (for the first or the umpteenth time) to "remain faithful to Jesus" (14:12).

QUESTIONS FOR READING 11:19–15:4 AGAIN

1. What message is being given by the opened temple (11:19)?

2. What is the Michael-episode (12:7–12) telling us?

3. How do we know who the two beasts of chapter 13 represent?

4. What is the message of chapter 14?

Chapter 5

The Tale of Two Cities: Part One
Revelation 15:5—19:10

WE MUST SURELY GET to see the End now! The printing press has made multiple runs across the page, bringing us to the End a number of times. We have seen life in this world from various angles: evils of human origin (the first five seals), natural disasters (the first four trumpets), supernatural evil directed at unbelievers (the fifth and sixth trumpets), and now supernatural evil directed at the whole world. Surely there can't be anything else to see, anything that would prevent us seeing the End. And yes, that is the subject of John's fourth vision. But it is not the End we might have been hoping for, although we should have been expecting it. The announcement in 11:15-18 had alerted us to the fact that God's full and final reign involves his wrath: the judging of the dead, and the destruction of the destroyers (11:18)—and this is what John sees now. This vision shows us the dark side of the End.

There is no way of avoiding the fact that this vision is dark. What John sees is very unpleasant and hard to take. But after what his third vision revealed, we must see these things. If our world is really like what we saw in 12:1-13:18, it would be unbearable if what we read here was not going to happen. Without these things, God would have abdicated, leaving the world without any moral order—no righting of great wrongs, no judgment of great evils, no vindication of what is good and true. So what is it that John gets to see now?

The Wrath of God

Once again, his vision begins with the sight of the temple being opened (15:5–8). Last time (11:19), it pointed us to God's mercy—his presence with his people, his covenant with his people, his rule over his people. But now it speaks of God's wrath, as the glory of his holiness is seen (15:8; cf. Isa 6:1–5). His glory and power are seen not only in the salvation of his people (7:10–12), but also in his judgment (19:1–2). We too easily forget this biblical balance between the kindness and sternness of God (Rom 11:22). If we do not remember that our God is a "consuming fire," we will not worship him acceptably, with reverence and awe (Heb 12:28–29)—and we will either treat his grace as weakness or else take it for granted as what we are entitled to.

We now get another group of seven angels (15:1, 6; cf. 8:2), this time with seven plagues. Each one is given a bowl filled with the wrath of God (15:7), and they take it in turns to pour them out (16:2–21). We can work out what this means by noting the parallels to other sections of Revelation and to parts of the Old Testament story.

We begin with the similarities to the seven trumpets. Like the first four trumpets, the first four bowls affect the land, the sea, fresh water, and the sun (16:2–9; cf. 8:7–12). The fifth bowl strikes the kingdom of the beast (16:10), reminding us of the fifth trumpet, which introduced the locusts who have the devil as their king (9:11). The sixth bowl is linked to the sixth trumpet by the reference to the river Euphrates (16:12; cf. 9:14). The seventh bowl results in a destructive earthquake (16:17–19), like that seen just before the seventh trumpet is sounded (11:13), only much more severe in its impact. This is true of the bowls as a group: unlike the trumpets, there is no limit to the harm that is done when each one is poured out.

There are also obvious similarities to the Egyptian plagues. The first bowl is like the plague of boils (Exod 9:8–12); the second and third are like that of Exodus 7:14–24; the fifth like the plague of darkness (Exod 10:21–23); the sixth like the plague of frogs (Exod 7:25–8:6); and the seventh like the plague of hail (Exod 9:13–26). And just as the Pharaoh remained hardhearted, so those afflicted by what is in the bowls refuse to repent (16:9, 11, 21).

The reference to the kings of the east coming from beyond the Euphrates (16:12) also sends us back to the Old Testament. It alludes to the way God used the military superpowers Assyria and Babylon as instruments of his judgment on his rebellious people (Isa 7:20; 8:5–8; Jer 20:4–6; 25:8–11).

There are links between the bowls and what John has seen in his previous vision. The first bowl points us back to 13:15–17, the fifth to 13:2, the sixth to 13:1–2, 11, 13, and the seventh to 14:9–10. Another important connection is found in the word translated "cursed" (16:9, 11, 21). This is the same word used of the sea beast in 13:5–6, where it is translated "blaspheme." Those who have given their allegiance to the beast go into judgment angrily shouting their defiance and hostility. You really do become like what you worship!

Finally, there is an important link between the events of the seventh bowl and those of the sixth seal (16:18, 20; cf. 6:12, 14). This is strengthened by the fact that the seven bowls are filled with the wrath of God (15:7), while the sixth seal introduces the "great day" of the wrath of God and the Lamb (6:16–17).

When we put all of this together, it is clear that the bowls depict final judgment. This explains the ways in which they are unlike the trumpets, which introduced preliminary judgments that were limited in their impact and intended to call people to repentance. But with the bowls, we have reached the dark side of the End. And just as we needed to see life before the End from several angles, so we also see the End itself from different perspectives. So one of the seven angels now comes to John in order to show him another way of seeing the End (17:1–2).

Babylon—did she fall or was she pushed?

As in 12:1–3, what John sees now is a woman and a beast (17:3–6). But there is a profound difference between these two visions, as this woman is anything but dignified and regal. She is in fact the original "scarlet woman"! Although dressed as a queen, she is "the great prostitute" (17:1). She has a cup filled with what is disgusting and depraved (17:4), and she is drunk—on Christian blood (17:6). She is seated on the beast, who turns out to be the sea beast of chapter 13 (17:3; cf. 13:1). The angel then offers an explanation of what John has just seen (17:7–18). Then John gets to hear three more voices. The first is a great angel, who announces the fall of Babylon for the second time (18:1–3; cf. 14:8). Then another heavenly voice describes Babylon's ruin (18:4–20). And finally, another great angel announces that Babylon's fall is complete and final (18:21–24). There are many echoes here of what the Old Testament prophets said about Babylon and the other nations that God used as instruments of judgment upon his unfaithful people.

What does all of this tell John and his churches about the End? First of all, what do we learn from the angel's words in chapter 17? These focus mostly on the beast, which (as we discovered in the previous vision) is a symbol for Satan and his activity. What the angel says about him indicates that he is using the same two methods that we have already seen in chapters 2 and 3 and chapters 12 and 13. The parody of God continues, as the beast "once was, now is not, and yet will come" (17:8)—an obvious allusion to the way God's eternal nature is stated (1:4, 8; 4:8). So the beast is God's rival, seeking to deceive—but however much he seeks to mimic God, he cannot be exactly like him. The purpose of the beast also continues: that is, making war (17:14; cf. 13:7; 16:14). Here the beast is God's enemy, seeking to destroy. Both strategies in Satan's modus operandi—fraud and force, trickery and tyranny—are in evidence here. But the alliance between the beast and the woman is destined to collapse (17:16). The kingdom of evil is built on hatred—and there can be no lasting bonds where hate holds sway.

What about the angel's references to eight kings (17:9–11) and ten kings (17:12)? Does this refer to our own time? Convinced that it does, because they think we are living in the End-times, some commentators search for possible parallels. Some years ago, they saw the ten kings as the European Community, which then consisted of ten nations. Unfortunately, this alliance then admitted more members! The problem here is not just that this approach was now wrong in fact, for it was always wrong in principle. The ten kings are not the European Community for the same reason that the locusts in chapter 9 are not helicopter-gunships. Revelation is written to the churches in Asia—and it means what it meant to them. But if it is speaking in code-language about our own time, what could it have meant for them—or for any other believers before us?

Seeking to take the "to them then" principle seriously, other commentators identify what John is seeing as the Roman Empire. This finds support in 17:9, for Rome was built on seven hills, and 17:18 can be understood this way. This approach has the distinct advantage of speaking to the seven churches about their world. Yet there are four problems with this view. First, the woman or city is filled with the blood not just of believers (17:6) but of all who have been killed on earth (18:24). This is not true of Rome, or of any one empire, no matter how evil. Secondly, this is part of a revelation of the End—and the Roman Empire has long since gone! Thirdly, this woman is the great city, which we met first in 11:8. There it is symbolically called Sodom, Egypt, and also Jerusalem—and now it is called Babylon (17:5). As we discovered in our study of chapter 11, this is a symbol for "the world," and so not just for Rome. Fourthly, second-time readers will know that this woman is the counterpart of a woman we will meet in the next vision. This one is the prostitute; that one is the bride of the Lamb (19:7). This is Babylon, the great city; that is the new Jerusalem, the holy city (21:2). So this one is the "kingdom of the world" (11:15), while that one is the kingdom of God. What John is seeing here is not Rome, but "the world."

We need to strike the right balance here. For the churches in Asia, the Roman Empire was the most obvious embodiment of what the Lord Jesus referred to as "the world." This explains the Roman coloring of the picture John is painting. But the world is not just "them over there." It is wherever unbelief rules—wherever God's Son is not loved and honored, and God's word is not welcomed and obeyed. So the dividing-line between Babylon and the new Jerusalem, between the kingdom of the world and the kingdom of God, does not lie between this nation and that, or this people and that, or this church and that. It runs through every nation, people, and church. Consider what we are told about the kings of the earth. They are allied with Satan (16:14, 16; 17:10–14), and are joined with Babylon in both her adulteries (17:2; 18:3) and her downfall (18:9–10)—and yet John sees them entering the holy city (21:24). And peoples, nations, and language-groups are hostile to God's witnesses (11:9–10), ruled by the beast (13:7), and allied with Babylon (17:15)—and yet they stand before the throne, rejoicing in salvation (7:9–10). In the seven letters (2:1–3:22), the Lord Jesus is giving strong warnings about ways in which the world has entered the churches. So anyone from anywhere may have a place in God's salvation and kingdom—and anyone from anywhere can and will end up outside in the darkness if they have not given their loyalty to Jesus.

Now we turn to see what we learn from the three voices in chapter 18. Why did Babylon fall (18:2)? And did she fall—or was she pushed? That is, was she destroyed by her own sins, or was she destroyed by God's judgment? What caused her to be "brought to ruin" (18:17, 19)? The answer lies in the cup she drinks. From one angle, the wine she consumes is her "adulteries" (17:2, 4; 18:3): she imbibes her own sins (18:6). From another angle, the wine in the cup is the wrath of God (16:19). What is this telling us? It means that there are two sides to God's judgment. When he removes his restraining hand, we receive in full the outcome of our sins. And all sin is inherently self-defeating: sin is an unstable compound, a black hole that is constantly imploding. It can only lead to ruin and bring us undone. So we see God's justice when the wicked are ensnared by the works of their own hands (Ps 9:16). On the other hand, Babylon's judgment is the outpouring of God's wrath upon her sin. All sin is culpable, deserving condemnation—and so God's judgment imposes a retribution that is just (19:2). So Babylon did fall: she imploded under the weight of her sins. And she was pushed: God poured out his wrath upon her. Both are true at the same time. This means that God's wrath is not vindictive rage, for judgment is the outworking of the inevitable consequences of sin. But nor is it an impersonal process, some kind of karma, for God visits his just judgment upon sinners and their sins.

This completes God's unmasking of evil, which he began in chapters 12 to 14. There Satan was revealed as a liar and a murderer who deceives and destroys. Now here we have seen how "utterly sinful" sin is (Rom 7:13). As we all know, it can often appear so attractive and desirable—but here, in the searchlight of God's holiness, it is shown up for what it is: a depraved and disgusting prostitute (17:3–6)! One of the functions of chapter 18 is to highlight several features of the world and its sinfulness. The first is its adulteries (18:3, 9; cf. 14:8; 17:2, 4). This is one of the ways Israel's prophets speak of her unfaithfulness—of giving to someone or something else the loyal love that belongs only to God (see, for example, Jer 3:6–14; Hos 1:2; 2:2–13; 3:1). The world works hard to siphon off our devotion, and to make itself the focus of our desires and ambitions. So we must work just as hard to avoid being corrupted by the world (2 Pet 1:4; 2:20). We must take care that we do not become God's enemies by becoming the world's friends (Jas 4:4). Secondly, we should note the world's excesses. We see this especially in its appetite for luxury (18:3, 7, 9, 11–14, 16). It is extravagant in the way it pampers itself, always grasping for more. Too much is never enough. This greed is idolatry: this relentless pursuit of mammon is the worship of a false god and an investment in the wrong treasure (Matt 6:19–20, 24; Col 3:5). Thirdly, there is its cruelty. It trades in human beings (18:13), treating people as cargo and as property, objects to be owned. And it sheds human blood in great quantities (18:24). It is particularly savage on those who proclaim God's word and those who believe it

(18:20, 24). Finally, there is its self-sufficient pride: "I sit enthroned as queen . . . I will never mourn" (18:7). The world is immensely smug, thoroughly self-satisfied and self-confident. In all of these ways—its adulteries, excesses, cruelty, and pride—it shows that it is ripe for judgment. This is the world setting itself up as a kingdom and thus rivalling and rejecting the kingdom of God. That is why it must be thrown down (18:21).

The Prostitute and the Bride

Once the fall of Babylon has been announced, John gets to hear two versions of the Hallelujah Chorus, each sounding like the roar of a vast assembly (19:1, 6). These four uses of "Hallelujah" (19:1, 3, 4, 6) are the only ones in the New Testament. So what has triggered off this praise and jubilation? The first of these two roars is a response to the dark side of the kingdom, to God's work of judgment (19:2). The second is a response to the bright side of the kingdom, to the triumph of the Lamb and the salvation of his people (19:6–9). We have no problem with this second one—but the first is difficult, for it sounds a bit too much like vindictive gloating (19:3). Is that what is happening here? To take it that way is to misread what the words in verses 1–3 are conveying. Far from gloating over Babylon's downfall, this is glorying in God's triumph. For judgment means the vindication of God's truth, which has been mocked, God's will, which has been defied, and God's character, which has been impugned. It also means the vindication of God's faithful but oppressed and persecuted people. "Hallelujah!" is the right response when God answers the most basic of all Christian prayers: "your kingdom come." And the coming of God's kingdom has a dark side: it means judgment as well as salvation. Before we leave this, we should also note that these Hallelujahs come only when the judgment is revealed to God's people. When judgment is announced to the world, it should be proclaimed with tears (Luke 19:41–44).

The second roar of "Hallelujah!" is also a response to the coming of God's kingdom (19:6). But this time it celebrates the alternative to judgment. At the End, there is not only the overthrow of Babylon, there is also the wedding of the Lamb (19:7). There is a stunning alternative to the great prostitute (17:1; 19:2)—the bride of the Lamb (19:7-8). The final coming of God's kingdom means great joy and gladness (19:7), for it means the perfection of the Lord Jesus' relationship with his church. It is this—the bright side of the kingdom—that John is now being made ready to see.

Before we leave it, let us recall where this fourth vision (15:5-19:10) has taken us. In essence, it does four things. First, it sounds a warning: "do not love the world" (1 John 2:15). It shows us that sin is deadly—and so we should have nothing to do with it! We learned in chapters 2 and 3 that some of the churches were compromising with evil, and so the Lord Jesus warned them of the danger they were in and called them to repent. That is also what this vision does—and we need this warning. It is all too easy to find sin attractive. Likewise, it is very easy not to recognize how deadly and destructive it really is, and how real and terrible judgment is. That is why the plagues John sees are so gruesome in their impact (16:2-21)—they are depicting the indescribable horror of being made by God and for God, and yet living against God and therefore being forever without God.

The second thing this vision does is to give us assurance. This world can be very daunting and discouraging for the believer. It can be fierce in its hostility and seductive in its duplicity. Either way, it can be difficult to resist. But John's vision of judgment tells us that evil does not have the last word. No matter how powerful and destructive it is, no matter how pervasive and successful it is, in the end sin will be overthrown. The kingdom of the world will not last (11:15). God will triumph. His kingdom will prevail. And this is what John is about to see in greater detail.

Thirdly, this vision serves as a reminder that our gospel is not authentic or complete unless we tell the truth about judgment (14:6-7). We need to remember that when he announced the coming of God's kingdom, Jesus did not call his hearers to rejoice, but to repent (Matt 4:17; Mark 1:14-15). Those who have given their loyalty to the kingdom of the world must be warned of its impending downfall and called to serve the true King before it is too late. So the idea that we should proclaim God's love without telling of his judgment is a serious error, because it leaves our hearers in grave danger. It also means misrepresenting the cross, which is not only where God's love shines most clearly but also where his judgment falls most heavily. In fact, the reason that the cross is the fullest display of his love—and of an utterly unique kind of love— is that that is where he turns his judgment upon himself so that we would not have to face it (1 John 4:10). We are free from judgment not because God's love excludes any such thing but only because God's love bears our judgment and exhausts it completely. As a result, we are offered a complete and permanent amnesty, freedom from all condemnation forever. However, if we refuse this amazing and immensely costly gift, then we must and will face final judgment. Our gospel must be as faithful in warning about God's wrath as it is joyful in holding out God's grace.

Fourthly, this vision confronts us with a very important challenge: am I as God-centered as I should be? Does it grieve me that in this world God's honor is slighted, his will flouted, his truth maligned, his grace spurned? Am I disturbed by the apparent ease with which the world, the flesh, and the devil have their way—and not only out there, but also in me? Do I therefore long and pray for the coming of God's kingdom, when everything will be put right— even though this means final judgment? Although the End will and must have this dark side, am I eager for God's final triumph, so that his glory will at last be fully displayed and properly acknowledged? Am I wanting the End just for my sake, or also for his sake?

Now that we have seen the End from this dark side, are we finally going to see its bright side? Now that we have seen the fall of Babylon, are we going to see the wedding of the Lamb? Are we about to see the coming of God's kingdom as full and final salvation? Yes, we are—but first . . .

Questions for Reading 15:5–19:10 Again

1. How do we work out what the seven bowls mean?
2. What connections are there between chapters 17 and 18?
3. What are the main points being made in chapter 18?
4. What are we meant to learn from the Hallelujah Chorus in chapter 19?

Chapter 6

The Tale of Two Cities: Part Two
Revelation 19:11—22:21

ONCE AGAIN, JOHN'S VISION begins with an opening in heaven—but this time, heaven itself is standing open (19:11). This means free access: the final barrier has been taken away, so there is now nothing to keep us out. It also means full disclosure, for there is nothing to keep heaven's secrets from view. It should now be possible for John to see everything that heaven contains—so what does he see as this final vision begins?

After the way the previous vision ends, we are expecting to see the Lamb and his bride in their wedding clothes (19:7). Instead we see a majestic royal warrior (19:11–16). Before the bride arrives (21:2), there are some final preparations that must be made. So who is this—and what does he need to do? Careful readers of Revelation will recognize at once that this is the Lord Jesus. The title, Faithful and True, takes us back to 3:14; the blazing eyes to 1:14; the sword from the mouth to 1:16; the quotation of Psalm 2:9 (v. 15) to 2:27; and the title, King of kings and Lord of lords, to 17:14. What John sees here is drawing our attention to four facts about Jesus. He is the Revealer, the Word of God (19:13). He not only testifies to God's word (1:5), he also embodies it. Everything that God has to say is summed up in Jesus Christ. He is God's message to the world. He is also the Redeemer. His robe is dipped in blood (19:13)—a way of taking us back to 1:5 and 5:9, and reminding us that he saves us by dying for us. Thirdly, he is the Ruler: the King of kings and Lord of lords (19:16) who rules the nations (19:15). He is sovereign over all of the world's powers and authorities. Finally, he is the Judge. He treads the winepress of God's wrath (19:15): that is, he puts God's righteous judgment into effect (14:19–20). But this Judge bears the marks of judgment upon himself: his robe is dipped in blood (19:13; cf. 14:20). The one who releases God's wrath upon the world has first taken it upon himself in the cross.

Why does John get to see Jesus like this at this point in his visions? This final appearance of Jesus is meant as a counterpart to the first one (1:12–18). Both of them are reassuring the churches that in all that happens to them, their Lord is in charge. Behind and underneath all of the complex and turbulent realities of our world (6:1–19:10) is one unshakeable fact: that Jesus is Lord. The seven churches need to know that he is far greater than all their foes—and we too need to be sure of this. So, no matter how hard-pressed they are, they remain utterly secure, for their Savior, our Savior, is sovereign..

The Final Showdown

What has Jesus come to do? What final preparations does he need to make before his bride can come for the wedding? John speci-fies two tasks: judging and making war (19:11). And this is what John now gets to see: the last battle (19:17–20:10) and then the last judgment (20:11–15).

The last battle has been foreshadowed in the previous vision (16:14, 16; 17:14)—but now we get to see it, not once but twice (19:17–21; 20:7–10)! Does this mean that there are two stages in the last battle? This is not very likely. What is more likely is that we are seeing the printing press in action once again, giving us two perspectives on this battle. This means that 20:1–6 is the press go-ing back to the beginning and running over the page once more. It is thus reminding us of one dimension of life in this world: namely, that Satan's power in the world is not absolute, but limited by God (20:3). He has been bound by the sovereign power of the Lord Jesus (20:2; cf. Mark 3:27). As a result, he is unable to deceive the nations (20:3): that is, he is unable to prevent the gospel from going to the nations and winning a vast multitude for God (7:9–10). The thousand years, like all the other periods of time in Revelation, is symbolic rather than literal: it stands for the time between the initial coming of God's kingdom (12:10) and the final coming of his kingdom (11:15). What we see in 20:7–10 is thus another side of God's work in overthrowing all evil at the End. This means the judgment and destruction of Babylon's sponsors and allies: the dragon (20:10) and the two beasts of chapters 12 and 13 (19:20).

When we take a closer look at the two passages dealing with the last battle, there is something of a surprise. There is no battle to see! We see the armies gathering, but there is no military engagement. Indeed, the armies of heaven are not equipped for war, but are dressed in their wedding finery (19:14; cf. 19:8). They are not expecting to fight, but to celebrate! What we do see is the forces of evil being defeated instantly and effortlessly. They are overcome by the sword from Jesus' mouth (19:21) and by fire from heaven (20:9). These are two pictures of God's word: for the sword, see Ephesians 6:17 and Hebrews 4:12; and for the fire, see Jeremiah 5:14 and 23:29. Martin Luther captured the point well in his great hymn, "A mighty fortress":

> And let the prince of ill look grim as e'er he will,
> he harms us not a whit: for why? His doom is writ;
> a word shall quickly slay him.

That is what John is seeing here: the powerful, authoritative word of the King of kings and Lord of lords effecting the complete overthrow of all the hosts of evil.

John now sees the throne again (20:11; cf. 4:2). This time it is the seat of judgment: the Emperor is acting as Judge. If God's rule is resisted, he will exercise it in judgment. Standing before the throne is every human being (20:12). Everyone is accountable to God—there are no exemptions: "we must all appear before the judgment seat" (2 Cor 5:10). In our world, there are many clever and powerful people who shout down the word of God—but God is going to have the last word! And his word will be perfectly fair, for we will all be judged by what we have done (20:12–13).

John gets to see all this after the last battle—so do these events happen one after the other? No, they don't, for the last battle and the last judgment are not two separate events, but two ways of looking at the same event: the coming of God's kingdom (11:15–18). So we are told that all people are destroyed in the battle (19:17–18), but then they appear in the court (20:12). John is seeing the dark side of the End from several different angles. The fall of Babylon, the last battle, and the last judgment are all ways of depicting God's overthrow of all evil when he brings in his kingdom. When John sees the armies, a military metaphor has sprung to life. Here sin is seen as defiance, the rejection of God's rule—and judgment thus means subduing rebellion. On the other hand, the court represents a legal metaphor, where sin is disobedience, transgressing God's will, and judgment means sentencing wickedness.

God has really labored this point! We have been seeing final judgment, the dark side of the kingdom, through chapters 16 to 20. Why does it need so much attention? In part, this is meant to reassure the seven churches. They are infected with evil on the inside and hard-pressed by evil from the outside. They need to know that no matter how terrible evil becomes, no matter how powerful it seems, God rules and he will rule forever. He will have the last word. This should be a source of relief and gratitude to all believers. We can join in this Hallelujah chorus: "Hallelujah! Salvation and glory and power belong to our God, for true and just are his judgments." (19:1–2). But this extensive coverage of final judgment is also meant as a warning for us. Everything that opposes God, defies his will, contradicts his holiness, will be destroyed. So every time sin raises its head, we should do a Joseph (Gen 39:12). The right response to sin is to flee from it!

The Kingdom of God

Now, at last, we get to see the bright side of the kingdom! So what does final salvation look like? What happens when the kingdom of the world becomes the kingdom of our Lord and of his Messiah (11:15)? John has two final visions which give us the answer. In the first, he sees two new realities: the new creation and the new Jerusalem (21:1–2). Then he hears two proclamations from the throne (21:3–4, 5–8). These sights and sounds are rich in symbolism, and contain many echoes of the Old Testament. As usual, the words interpret the pictures. What do they tell us here?

The first point made by the words John hears is that *God's purpose is now complete*. We see this in several ways. First, his foundational covenant-promise has now reached its fullest fulfillment. Now God is truly present with his people as their God (21:3; cf. Gen 17:7; Exod 6:7). Secondly, his great promises concerning the salvation of the End-time are now fulfilled. So John sees the promised new creation (21:1; cf. Isa 65:17; 66:22). Isaiah's promise equates the new creation with the new Jerusalem (Isa 65:17–19). This tells us that John is not seeing two realities but one: God's kingdom as the new creation and the new Jerusalem (21:1–2). He also hears that what Isaiah promised about final salvation—the end of death and the wiping away of all tears (Isa 25:7–9)—has now occurred (21:4). Thirdly, just as "It is done!" marks final judgment (16:17), it also marks final salvation (22:6). This does not mean that judgment and salvation have equal weight in God's final purpose, any more than death and life are equally ultimate. Final judgment means the second death (20:6, 14; 21:8), but final salvation means everlasting life (21:6; 22:1–2, 17). We have reached the Omega-point, the End (21:6), not when we get to judgment but when we get to the new creation.

The second point made in these proclamations from the throne is that *God's presence with his people is now direct and permanent*. There is no longer any separation between heaven and earth, between God's realm and our domain (Ps 115:16), because "God's dwelling place is now among the people, and he will dwell with them" (21:3). Heaven was God's dwelling place (Ps 33:13–14), but now heaven and earth have become one. God is where we are—and we are where God is. That is not because we have gone to heaven, which is the way we usually think about the End. Rather, it is because heaven has come to us (21:2, 10). God has taken the initiative to bring us together, to remove the barrier separating heaven and earth. The wedding has come, so the bride and her husband will no longer be separated. They are now united permanently. Distance has been replaced by intimacy: once we saw "only a reflection as in a mirror," but now "we shall see face to face" (1 Cor 13:12; cf. 22:4).

The third point these proclamations make is that *God's people have now entered into full and final salvation.* We see this in the first two points above. We see it also in the reference to those whose thirst is quenched by the water of life (21:6). This takes us back to 7:16–17, part of John's first vision of final salvation. We see it again in the reference to those who are "victorious" (21:7). In the messages to the seven churches (2:1–3:22), promises of ultimate salvation are made to these victors. Now John is seeing the form that this salvation takes. Next, the reference to God's children and heirs (21:7) reminds us of Romans 8:17–21, with its vision of the whole creation made new and glorious at the End. What Paul envisages there, John now gets to see. Finally, the mention of those who go down into final judgment (21:8) forms a deliberate contrast with this depiction of final salvation.

Life in the City of God

John now gets to see the holy city at some length. This is the kingdom of God, the glorious counterpart to the doomed kingdom of this world (11:15). It is shown to him by the same guide who took him to see the great prostitute (21:9–10; cf. 17:1–3). This time his guide invites him to see the Lamb's bride—but what he actually sees is the holy city, the new Jerusalem (21:9–10). These two are one and the same—just as the prostitute is the great city, Babylon the great (17:1, 5). Let this be a final reminder—just in case we still need one!—that as we read Revelation we are not watching a documentary, a video that shows us the future. We are reading John's report of his visions of the word of God (1:2)—and so we get to see imagery that has been animated, word-pictures that have sprung to life.

John's attention is directed first to the construction of the holy city (21:11–21). Three of its features are especially important. First, the city perfectly embodies and expresses the glory of God (21:11). Now at last, God's glory is fully revealed; now at last it is embodied in a way that filters none of it out and holds none of it back. This city is ablaze with the beauty, the purity, the majesty of God. Secondly, the city represents perfection. Hence its shape: it is a perfect cube (21:16). And it has been constructed out of the most precious materials possible (21:18–21). Thirdly, one of its most important perfections, one of the principal ways in which it displays God's glory, has to do with the gates and foundations of the city wall. The twelve gates represent the twelve tribes of Israel (21:12), and the twelve foundations stand for the Lamb's apostles (21:14). In other words, this city symbolizes the unity of the people of God under both the old and new covenants. One of the chief reflections of the glory of God is that at the End, all of the redeemed gather before his throne (7:9–10, 14).

After John has noted these features of the city, his attention is then directed to its contents (21:22–22:5). His report of what he saw contains many allusions to the Old Testament, for this city represents the complete and final fulfillment of all the promises and purposes of God. His report also contains links with other sections of the book. Most of what was promised to the "victorious" in the seven church-messages (2:1–3:22) is seen in the city. And the sneak preview of final salvation in 7:15–17 is here confirmed and expanded. Reading this vision in light of all these allusions and links will pay rich dividends. But here we have room only to note the most important features of what John saw.

John is struck first of all by what the city does not contain. The city has no temple (21:22), because God is fully and eternally present (21:3). There is thus no need for the building that symbolized

God's presence with his people (Exod 25:8; 29:44–46; 1 Kgs 8:10–13). The substance has now replaced the symbol. Secondly, the city has no sunlight or moonlight (21:23) and no night (21:25; 22:5), for God's glory—his radiant splendor—will be fully displayed (cf. Isa 60:1–3). Thirdly, there is no longer any curse (22:3), for there is no more need for judgment. That is because the Lamb has shed his blood for us (1:5; 5:9; 7:14; 12:11). And because he bore our curse in his death (Gal 3:13), it has gone from us forever. The permanent exclusion of any judgment is also due to the fact that no sin will ever enter this city (21:27) for those who are committed to sin are shut outside (22:15). All of those who live in the city are not only free from any condemnation for sin, having washed their robes in the blood of the Lamb (22:14; cf. 7:14), but are also free from any contamination by sin. They are entirely free not only of sin's penalty but also of its presence and power, holy people who will continue to be holy and nothing but holy (22:11). That is why they can live in the presence of the God who is completely and utterly holy (4:8). Finally, because there is no sin or death there, there will be no grief or pain and thus no tears in this city (21:4). Because the only way into the city is through the "great tribulation," the ordeal of life in this fallen and godless world (7:14), we will all bring many tears with us—but with great tenderness and compassion, God will wipe every one of them from our eyes (7:17; 21:4). Instead of pain and sorrow, we will know only deep comfort and intense joy.

Then what does the city contain? The first and most fundamental answer is that God is there, in all his glory (21:23) and royal majesty (22:1, 3). It is his presence that makes it new and wonderful. Secondly, this city is bursting with life. And now there is nothing to impede or challenge this life, for death is dead and gone (20:14; 21:4)! The center of the city is occupied by the river of life (22:1–2) and the tree of life (22:2). This tells us two things. The first is that life in the kingdom will be the opposite of life in this world. Here, our life progresses inevitably downwards towards death. As we age, our vigor fades, our capacities diminish, and our horizons shrink. But it is life, not death, that rules in God's city. So there we will become more and more alive all the time—more robust, more dynamic, more capable. Instead of shrinking, our horizons will keep on expanding, and our capacities will keep pace with them. Secondly, the presence of the tree of life tells us that this city is paradise restored, a new Eden (Gen 2:9). But it is much more than that. The world's kings bring their splendor into it (21:24), and it contains the glory and honor of the nations (21:26). Obviously, the fall of Babylon and the destruction of the world's kings (19:19, 21) is not the whole story. Those human works that express rebellion against God should and will go down into judgment—but everything that was done for love of God will come into his city. So God will not simply go back to the beginning and reestablish the garden of Eden, as though the whole of human history has been a complete waste of time. The Bible's story starts with a garden but ends with a garden-city. This is not the product of our ambitions and activities, a new Babel (Gen 11:4). It is God who is the architect and builder of this city (Heb 11:10), which is why John sees it coming down out of heaven from God (21:3, 10). Yet the way God builds it is to incorporate whatever has been done to honor him into its fabric, thus preserving everything that is truly good and right and beautiful. So part of the comfort held out to dying Christians is that "their deeds will follow them" (14:13)—into the city. No "work produced by faith" or "labor prompted by love" (1 Thess 1:3) is ever lost or wasted or fruitless, for it will have its place in the coming kingdom. And this will at last reveal the true nobility of humble and faithful service, as everything that has been done for Jesus adds its own special radiance to all the other glories of this city.

What happens in the heavenly city? What will we do there? John learns first that we will serve the enthroned Emperor and his Lamb (22:3; cf. 7:15). So heaven is not a celestial retirement village—we will not spend eternity desperately trying to fend off boredom by playing endless games of Scrabble and carpet bowls! What lies ahead of us is activity that matters, because it will be done for the God who has loved us and saved us. He will give us the gift of significance by giving us the privilege of service. Secondly, we will see God's face (22:4). When the sixth seal was broken

(6:12–17), we discovered that this prospect filled unbelievers with such terror that they wanted to be crushed to death (6:16). But believers have always longed to see the face of God (Num 6:24–26; Pss 27:8; 80:3, 7, 19; 105:4). For us, there can be no greater joy than the prospect of direct and unbroken intimacy with the God we have known only partially and loved very poorly in this life—and that is what we will have in his heavenly kingdom. Because there will be nothing to hinder our access to him, all of his glories and excellencies will be on full and open display. These are not only utterly pure and good but also stunningly beautiful, so that we will not find them forbidding in any way, but will instead have an intense desire to drink them in. And since they are also limitless, even an eternity of adoring contemplation will leave us feeling like novices who have hardly begun to see all that God is. In the presence of such a God, boredom is simply not a possibility! Thirdly, we will reign with him (22:5): our service of him will mean sharing his rule. So what we do will not be menial or meaningless, for we will at last fulfill our calling to exercise dominion over the works of God's hands (Gen 1:28; Ps 8:6–8). Under God, we will rule over the new creation. What lies ahead of us, therefore, is great nobility and great responsibility—and because we will become more alive all the time, we will at last be able to live up to such a high calling.

Why has John been allowed to see all of this and tell us about it? What impact is this vision of God's kingdom meant to have on us? One of the most important effects it should have is to give us a better way of envisaging what lies beyond our death. This seems to be a problem for most Christian people. We know that the Bible tells us that to depart and be with Christ is "better by far" (Phil 1:23)—but we seem to have great difficulty believing this. A big part of the problem appears to lie in our imaginations. When we try to picture what lies ahead of us, most of us struggle. We know that life beyond death is not just a re-run of this life—but we find it difficult to come up with a clear alternative. It seems that the best most of us can do is to picture a disembodied soul, like a piece of porous cling-wrap wafting about in the heavenly breezes! The problem is that what we see on our mental screens is something much less real that what we have now—an emaciated, anemic kind of existence. No wonder we don't look forward to it! But John's pictures are pointing us in the opposite direction. They are telling us that we are headed for something that is much more real than what we have now. Life in God's city will not deprive us of anything real and good. Instead, we will be immeasurably and endlessly enriched. We will become more and more alive all the time (22:1–2), as we revel not only in all the glories of human civilization (21:24, 26) but in all the glory of God (21:11, 23). This is an End that means more . . . and more . . . and more! If we keep coming back to what John tells us here and chewing over what it means, we will begin to see just how desirable it really is—a new kind of life that is truly "better by far" (Phil 1:23).

This points us to another reason John got to see all of these things. By showing us the glories of his city, this vision points us to the excellencies of its architect and builder (Heb 11:10). The more clearly we grasp how magnificent life in God's new world will be, the more fully we will recognize the greatness and grace of a God who planned it, then promised it to his people, paid a terrible price for it ("the blood of the Lamb"), and brought it to completion despite the furious and devious opposition of the kingdom of the world and the evil upstart who rules it. Such a God should be praised and loved and served wholeheartedly and forever, not only by his courtiers (4:9–10), but by everyone without exception (5:13). That is where this last part of John's final vision should take us. So I need to ask you, is that what it has done for you?

And with that, we have almost come to the end of Revelation. Its final section (22:6–21) does three things. First, it reminds us of the book's fourfold character, as a revelation by God of what must soon take place (22:6), a testimony by John (22:8), a prophecy (22:7, 10, 18–19), and a letter to churches (22:21; cf. 1 Thess 5:28; 2 Thess 3:18).

Secondly, and more importantly, it enables us to hear again several voices that we must listen to. We have John's final words (22:8, 17b–19, 20b–21) and those of his angelic guide (22:6, 9–11). We also hear what the Lord Jesus says (22:7, 12–16, 20a), reminding us for the final time who he is and how we should respond to him. And then we have the words of the Spirit and the bride (22:17a), showing us what we too should be saying in response to the promise and reassurance we have in Jesus' words. The chief function of this chorus of voices is to remind us of "the things that must soon take place" (22:7, 12, 20), and of how to respond to the message of Revelation in light of this fact.

Thirdly, and most importantly, this concluding section focuses our attention on the Lord Jesus Christ. It announces his coming (22:7, 12, 20), reminds us of his greatness (22:13, 16), and commends us to his grace (22:21). It thus forms an important counterpart to the beginning of the book, which emphasizes his greatness (1:5-7) and then depicts his glory (1:12-18). He is the First and the Last, the Beginning and the End (22:13)—our foundation and our destination, our basis and our goal. And he must be our focus, now and always. In dealing with the past, in coping with the present, in facing the future, we must be firmly centered upon Jesus Christ—and in reading Revelation too, we must be firmly centered upon him. We must take great care—in living our lives and in reading this book—not to be distracted from him or centered somewhere else. If our reading of Revelation has not brought us to him again and again, we have not been reading it rightly.

Questions for Reading 19:11–22:21 Again

1. Why does this final vision begin with an appearance by the Lord Jesus?

2. What is the meaning of what John sees in 19:17–20:15?

3. What are we meant to learn from John's vision of the holy city?

4. How is 22:6–21 meant to guide us in reading Revelation?

What Next?

Now that you have finished working your way through Revelation, how can you build on what you have learned? One very good way of doing this is to find someone who will read it with you, so that you can share with them what you have discovered. This will not only help you to remember things you don't want to forget, but it will also be a real encouragement to them. And if they get excited about seeing the gospel presented in such a vivid and powerful way, they are likely to want to pass this on to someone else. This will mean that, bit by bit, Revelation is taking the place in our lives that it ought to have. And that can only do us good.

Another good way of taking the next step is to work your way through Revelation with a commentary or a guidebook that gives you more detail than this one. Here are some suggestions about good books you could use. Any of those in the first group would make a good next step after you have finished this book. Those in the second group are more detailed and thorough, but not as comprehensive as bigger, more technical commentaries.

Paul Gardner, *Revelation: The Compassion and Protection of Christ* (Focus on the Bible: Christian Focus, 2001).

Vern S. Poythress, *The Returning King: A Guide to the Book of Revelation* (P&R, 2000).

Steve Wilmshurst, *The Final Word: Revelation Simply Explained* (Welwyn Commentary: Evangelical Press, 2008).

Gordon D. Fee, *Revelation* (New Covenant Commentary: Cascade, 2011).

James M. Hamilton Jr., *Revelation: The Spirit Speaks to the Churches* (Preaching the Word: Crossway, 2012).

Dennis E. Johnson, *Triumph of the Lamb: A Commentary on Revelation* (P&R, 2001).

James L. Resseguie, *The Revelation of John: A Narrative Commentary* (Baker, 2009).

Michael Wilcock, *The Message of Revelation* (The Bible Speaks Today: IVP, 1975).

If you do make use of some of these books, you will find that they do not agree with each other at every point. I hope you won't let this discourage you. Instead, use this as an opportunity to read Revelation again, just as carefully and prayerfully as you have done before. Then see if you can work out which of the differing interpretations seems to do more justice to everything that John tells us. If you aren't sure which view to follow, you could see what a more detailed commentary says about the relevant passage or ask the opinion of a friend who knows the Bible better than you do. Or you could just leave the matter unresolved for now, and come back to it later after you have had more time to mull it over. Whichever choice you make, it is always helpful to remind yourself of everything about the message of Revelation you can be sure about. This is a good way of ensuring that instead of getting caught up in lots of detail, you give most attention to what is most important. It is vital that you maintain a clear view of the gospel pageant with the Lord God and the Lamb at the head of the procession.

The best overall guide to what the Bible teaches us about the future is Eckhard Schnabel, *40 Questions about the End Times* (Kregel, 2011). This includes a helpful discussion of many issues to do with the interpretation of Revelation.

The most important way that you can take the next step is to incorporate what you have learned into the way you pray. This will then spill over into the way you live with God and for God. So now that you have finished this book, why not read through Revelation again? On this journey through the book, make a note of everything that can give shape and focus to your praying—everything that you can thank God for or ask him about, every promise you can rejoice in or warning that you must heed, every verse that gives you good words to use in speaking to God.

So now we have come to the end of our journey. When we set off, you may have been a little apprehensive about what you were letting yourself in for. I hope that we have avoided all of the problems and pitfalls that might have been worrying you, and that you are very glad you decided to take the plunge and make the journey. I hope that what we have done has given the book of Revelation back to you, so that it does not need to be ignored as a troublesome alien but can now play its role alongside all of the other books in the New Testament. And this means that I am hoping that you have been gripped in a new way by the grandeur of the gospel of salvation, the gospel of God's kingdom—and that you have therefore seen the glory and grace of our sovereign Savior in a way that has left you "lost in wonder, love, and praise." This will ensure that when you put this book away and close your Bible, you will head back into our lost and needy world more determined than ever to make your life count for the sake of Jesus.

www.ingramcontent.com/pod-product-compliance
Lightning Source LLC
Chambersburg PA
CBHW071105090426
42737CB00013B/2489